The Authorities

Powerful Wisdom from Leaders in the Field

SUE JEFFERSON
Gender Balance & Win

©2016 by 10-10-10 Publishing

All rights reserved. No part of this publication may be reproduced or transmitted in any form or by any means, electronic or mechanical, including photocopying, recording, or any other information storage and retrieval system without the written permission of the publisher and author.

Published by:
10-10-10 PUBLISHING
MARKHAM, ON
CANADA

Printed in the United States of America.
ISBN:

FOREWORD

Experts are to be admired for their knowledge, but they often remain unrecognized by the general public because they save their information and insights for paying customers and clients. There are many experts in a given field, but their impact is limited to the handful of people with whom they work.

Unlike experts, authorities share their knowledge and expertise far more broadly, so they make a big impact on the world. Authorities become known and admired as leading experts and, as such, typically do very well economically and professionally. Most authorities are also mature enough to know that part of the joy of monetary success is the accompanying moral and spiritual obligation to give back.

Many people want to learn and work with well-respected and generous authorities, but don't always know where to find them. They may be known to their peers, or within a specific community, but have not had the opportunity to reach a wider audience. At one time, they might have submitted a proposal to the For Dummies or Chicken Soup for the Soul series of books, but it's now almost impossible to get accepted as a new author in such branded book series.

It is more than fitting that Raymond Aaron, an internationally known and respected authority in his own right, would be the one to recognize the need for a new venue in which authorities could share their considerable knowledge with readers everywhere. As the only author ever to be included in both of the book series mentioned above, Raymond has had the opportunity to give back and he understands how crucial it is for authorities to have a platform from which to share their expertise.

I have known and worked with Raymond for a number of years and consider him a valued friend and talented coach. He knows how to spot talented and knowledgeable people and he desires to see them prosper. Over the years, success coaching and speaking engagements around the world have made it possible for Raymond to meet many of these talented authorities. He recognizes and relates to their passion and enthusiasm for what they do, as well as their desire to share what they know. He tells me that's why he created this new nonfiction branded book series, *The Authorities*.

Dr. Nido Qubein
President, High Point University

TABLE OF CONTENTS

Introduction...V

Gender Balance & Win..1
Sue Jefferson

Branding Small Business....................................21
Raymond Aaron

Happiness: How to Experience the "Real Deals"..............35
Marci Shimoff

Sex, Love and Relationships................................45
Dr. John Gray

Break Through Your Barriers & Live Your Dreams.............51
Sandra Westland

Honor Your Inner Treasures.................................61
Celina Tio

Have More Money, More Clients and More Freedom
by Going Digital...81
Ashar Alam

Create the Life of Your Dreams.............................89
Dexter Montgomery & Pamela Montgomery

Enter Into a Passionate Relationship with Your Own Life....99
Silvana L. Avram

Evolution of Consciousness for the Entrepreneur...........115
Audree Tara Weitzman

Declutter Your Mind For Success...........................127
Erin Muldoon Stetson

Control Money Before it Controls You......................141
K. Raj Singh

ACKNOWLEDGEMENTS

My mother & father. Pioneers in their pursuits, showing how they always faced their obstacles and providing me with many insights of people in the world of business.

Nick Vermont (CEO, McCain Foods GB Ltd.). One of the most astute, bold and visionary business leaders I know, from whom I learned so much about boardroom dynamics and leadership. For his sponsorship of me into business critical roles and recognising the transformations created. We had a blast!

Tim Seeton (Managing Partner, ParaComm International). One of the world's pioneers in organisational coaching and business transformation. For his generosity in sharing the power of the right conversations so step changing teamwork and achieving unprecedented results. I am privileged to be your friend and colleague.

Alastair Paton (Managing Partner, UK and Regional Director EMEA, Signium). Not only an exceptional head-hunter but one with unique and far-reaching insight into the challenges facing boardrooms and executives today.

Stuart Herd (Commercial Director, McCain Foods) and **Ross Hunter** (Supply Chain Director, McCain Foods) As experts in their field, for sharing their range of experiences of leadership and dynamics in different boardrooms.

Daniel and **Matthew**. My two boys who keep me grounded with their different perspectives of all things in the world and my parenting/management approach.

Celia Lashlie (Author of He'll Be OK), Whose insights into teenage boys and men have opened my eyes to significantly better understanding and as a consequence, re-shaped my own behaviour.

Lady Barbara Judge (Chair of Institute of Directors). For sharing her career journey, stories and commitment to women in business, inspiring me to keep making an impact developing gender balanced leadership in the workplace.

Dr. John Gray (author of *Men are from Mars, Women are from Venus*). From first helping me understand how we think differently to now sharing a stage as Authorities in this field, his pioneering has enabled me to help business men and women unlock their full potential.

INTRODUCTION

This book introduces you to *The Authorities* — individuals who have distinguished themselves in life and in business. Authorities make a big impact on the world. Authorities are leaders in their chosen fields. Authorities typically do very well financially, and are evolved enough to know that part of the joy of monetary success is the accompanying social, moral and spiritual obligation to give back.

Authorities are not just outstanding. They are also *known* to be outstanding.

This additional element begins to explain the difference between two strategic business and life concepts — one that seems great, but isn't, and the other that fills in the essential missing gap of the first.

The first concept is "the expert."

What is an expert? The real definition is ...

EXPERT: *a person who knows stuff*

People who have attained a very senior academic degree (like a PhD or an MD) definitely know stuff. People who read voraciously and retain what they read definitely know stuff. Unfortunately, just because you know stuff does not mean that anyone respects the fact that you do. Even though some experts are successful, alas, most are not — because knowing stuff is not enough.

Well, then, what is the missing piece?

What the expert lacks, "the authority" has. The authority both knows stuff and is *known* to know stuff. So, more simply ...

AUTHORITY: *a person who is known as an expert*

The difference is not subtle. The difference is not merely semantic. The difference is enormous.

When it comes to this subject, there are actually three categories in which people fall:

- People who don't know much and are unsuccessful in life and in business. Most people fall in this category.

- People who know stuff, but still don't leave much of a footprint in the world. There are a lot of people like this.

- Experts who are also *known* as experts become authorities and authorities are always wondrously successful. Authorities are able to contribute more to humanity through both their chosen work and their giving back.

This book is about the highest category, *The Authorities* — people who have reached the peak in their field and are known as such.

You will definitely know some of The Authorities in this book, especially since there are some world-famous ones. Others are just as exceptional, but you may not yet know about them. Our featured author, for example, is Sue Jefferson. If you or a loved one have been diagnosed with cancer, you must read Gender Balance & Win. In this chapter, you will learn seven all-natural remedies to help fight cancer. Yvonne shares her research so that you can make informed decisions on treatment, should you ever need it or know of anyone that does.

To be considered for inclusion in a subsequent edition of *The Authorities*, register to attend a future event at www.aaron.com/events where you will be interviewed and considered.

VIII

Gender Balance & Win

SUE JEFFERSON

THE CHALLENGE FOR MEN AND WOMEN IN BUSINESS TODAY

Today's world of business has come a long way though it is still lagging behind in gender bias.

As a woman how do you navigate this issue and ensure success in your workplace, become an exceptional leader and love both your work and your home life?

As a leader, male or female, how do you enable your organisation to become naturally inclusive, overcoming the unconscious bias that commonly exists?

Many successful companies have adopted programs to recognize talented women, create an inclusive culture and are designed to nurture their success driven employees. This is a wise move for companies looking to make an impact as these high achieving individuals can have an enormous positive effect on business results.

The reasons why diversity & gender balance brings better business performance are obvious – they bring breadth of thinking to every leadership team. However, biases and barriers can still exist even in the most innovative and progressive companies, particularly if they are quite male orientated. These barriers manifest either as unconscious bias; emotional reasons that are not recognised as such, or with a limited few, still conscious bias that are now simply hidden under the auspices of legislation, but don't let that be an excuse for what's holding you back.

This chapter, compiled from listening to and reading the very many different viewpoints of business leaders, head hunters, men and women, as well as my own experiences as a Boardroom executive who has delivered unprecedented growth, seeks to offer those leaders of companies with an unconscious bias together with their HR Directors, a way to recognise barriers in their organisation, practical solutions to overcome them and how to get started in creating and benefiting their business with gender balance in their workplace.

A PRACTICAL SOLUTION FOR LEADERS AND INDIVIDUALS

Using my 30 years work experience, where I became one of the first female Director/VPs in a global food manufacturer, leading multi-discipline teams and transforming business outcomes, all while maintaining a marriage of 24 years and raising a family, I have created a toolkit called the C.A.R.B.O.N. Way to Transform to Sparkling Success©. I now work with visionary organisations to enable their high potential women to develop simple to apply strategies & support leaders to constructively address these barriers and provide practical applications to enable mutual success and career/life balance.

First of all, what is this toolkit that I talk about? Known as the C.A.R.B.O.N. Way to Transform to Sparkling Success© with six key pieces, addressing the most common barriers holding back women and organisations.

Cutting Through To Be Heard: If you are not heard by your colleagues and superiors in the workplace it will be difficult to achieve any level of success. Before you do anything you must first be heard.

Influencing Action - Getting the right actions from the right people: Once you have caught the right ear you need them not to just listen but also put your words into action. Without action you cannot move forward and accomplish goals.

Resilience - Responding to Setbacks: You are going to face them and the higher you go, the more you'll have, and the more significant they will be. Setbacks happen to everyone but it's how you respond to them that matter and pave the road to success in both work and life.

Resilience - Building your Mental Toughness: Underlying resilience is an important asset in today's competitive business world. As moving up in the workplace and standing out in the crowd becomes harder, mental toughness will give you the ability and advantage to stay strong, balanced and be an inspiring leader.

Creating Awesome Self Belief: This is something that I find alongside Cutting Through to Be Heard and Influencing Others, that women struggle with the most. Being skilled in this, is the backbone to enjoying work everyday, being bold to make a difference in your organisation and having the ability to develop others.

Setting Outcomes and Wowing People - As you deliver unprecedented results and inspire others to deliver too: Most people do not think ahead to outcomes but just focus on the tasks to be done. It is much more powerful if you start with the end in mind, determine what is missing to achieve this and then plan the right deliverables. It's faster, more likely to secure success and engages people to deliver for you. At a mastery level this will enable you to transform everything you touch.

Our Needs: Knowing the human needs that drive behaviour and how to use them. This is important because these unconscious needs underpin everything you do and everything that other people do. Understanding these, means you can enable your own and others' needs to be satisfied, feel fulfilled and so sparkle inside and out.

So that's the C.A.R.B.O.N. model©.

For maximum impact and embedding new ways of working, I bring the model to life as an in-house workshop for organisations who want to develop their high performing, high potential talent. If you keep these concepts in mind through the rest of the chapter where we discuss the barriers women face, the unconscious barriers holding back leaders and how to address them, I have no doubt in my mind that you will find the mutual success you are seeking. I look forward to every woman in an organisation using these concepts and becoming a sparkling diamond very soon.

UNLOCKING PROVEN BUSINESS BENEFITS FROM GENDER BALANCE

Technology is changing the world and how we view it, quicker than ever before, from employment to leisure and transportation to education. With such rapid change, as customers change the dynamics of business rules and organisations struggle to maintain growth, why are more leaders not tapping into a proven source of greater performance?

A source that McKinsey & co. stated is worth an additional $12 trillion of business, in their May 2016 report "Women Matter: The business and economic case for gender diversity" Technological moves over the next 15 to 20 years will bring a wave of changes that will fundamentally change our careers. This $12 trillion opportunity comes on the back of gender balance within the world of work, where gender gaps in our society are closely tied with improvement of access to areas that could unlock economic opportunities for women.

However, barriers do exist. It has been said, the danger of the modern gender workplace bias is that too often it can seem like no problem at all. The disappearance of explicit sexism can give the false impression that it no longer exists. Studies spanning over the last few decades indicate gender bias not only exists but thrives in male dominated professions. A woman meant to be a leader, will stand her ground where she pushes through this narrow minded viewpoint that they are second class citizens and sometimes wins, proving her worth. Astounding research results reports this stereotype gender bias is thriving and the experiential evidence is additionally overwhelming. Many actions have been uncovered that women can take to position themselves for the career advancements they have worked for and deserve. Although stressful for a woman in the workplace they need to be aware of the negative gender stereotypes found in most job markets surrounding them. When they make their career decisions they need to anticipate the biases some of these stereotypes foster; and they need to manage the impressions they make to avoid or overcome these biases. Women, as well as men need to know what their desired outcome is and pursue it in whichever manner necessary to achieve their goals.

Performance and business success research has taken the focus and attention into the female entrepreneurship field although there is still much controversy on how to measure performance. This is over which indicators should be taken into account, but mainly when there are comparative studies between men and women entrepreneurs. This ludicrous controversy in today's world seems even more difficult to imagine as it is sexist but exists. At its essence, it is about the success of a company. Posing the quandary of whether a company can be successful if they are created by women, or have a higher rate of failure or lower performance in comparison with those created by men.

Economic performance studies have used variable ways to measure it between the women and men, without considering other type of measurements that can be important for women entrepreneurs, apart from the economic ones. However, when researched using more than the economic results of performance it has been argued that male and female entrepreneurs pursue different business goals. Entrepreneurial women generally emphasize social goals, while male entrepreneurs emphasize economic goals.

Research studies conducted tell us that companies with at least one woman on the board outperform those companies that had no women. They indicate blue-chip companies with at least one woman on the board outperform others with no women by 26%. The study was done over a six-year measurement by Credit Suisse (Credit Suisse Group is a Swiss multinational financial services.) Studies also show results that the difference made by women during the financial crisis was particularly noticeable. New growth was strong in mid-decade as there was little difference in share-price performance between companies but by 2008 after the financial crisis (2007-2008) stocks with women on the board have strongly surged ahead. It is reported by securities research and analytics that greater gender diversity is a valuable additional metric to the financials, when evaluating investments.

Another astounding indicator, where studies over a six year period reported an average return on equity of 16% with companies that had women on the board vs. 12% from those that had none. These same companies with women reported the income grew 14% on average over companies with no women on the board at 10%.

Further investigation into outstanding business performances and gender bias find that there is a large opportunity cost for companies associated with male-only executive boards. Like a world still addicted to fossil fuels, these companies are suffering now. The conclusion drawn is that those businesses stuck in the past are not fully unlocking their growth potential.

In today's fast changing environment, large companies need to find ways to become agile, understanding and responding to the dynamic needs of their customers and delivering the best solutions ahead of far reaching competitors. Frankly, without gender balance and diversity, those organisations will become case study dinosaurs.

It is clear from this evidence that gender balance makes smart business sense.

Business management teams at all levels need to change from limited Group Think to broader thinking and can do so by better leveraging their hidden advantage with their female employees. Some obvious benefits from gender balance include smarter understanding of fifty percent of purchasers (the females): their issues, their needs, their drivers for response. Intuitive understanding of employees and their needs enables better communication, engagement and support for ongoing change. Broader diverse experience enables people to see challenges differently – identifying different risks and creating different solutions.

The final advantage is that by working in a collaborative way and delegating outcomes not simply tasks, results can be achieved at a better pace.

A significant benefit of gender balance is that these improvements often come from employees already within their system. There will be hidden talent within everyone's current organisation – women who know the business, systems, the people, the vision, how the company works. Some of these women will be evident in the talent review picture as high performing and high potential people. So once unlocked, given the right opportunity and support, they will hit the ground running and your organisation will see improved performance within months.

Additionally, the natural behaviour that arises from gender balance is improved collaboration – seeking to find win-win situations, building on others' ideas and putting the company success ahead of their own. Including female employees in decision making, replacing dated Command and Control management methods, is a necessary requirement for an organisation to leverage the maximum of benefits from their employees. Not only will gender balance and collaboration improve morale across every level of management team, the cultural change will start to subdue some of the behaviours seen between ambitious executives which leads to the fragility of the boardroom which is a challenge for most CEOs to manage.

As organisations see improved prosperity, risks better managed, stronger morale and commitment, they benefit from a natural cultural shift which will create better team working and an agility to act in a way that every large organisation desires if they are to successfully respond in this fast changing world. A more accommodating workplace, enabling work and life integration and balance, is becoming a must for the new generation, male and female, therefore a company that embraces this now will not only benefit from the immediate advantages but will be advantageously placed to secure the best talent going forward. Equally they will embrace diversity and be a natural global player, attracting customers across cultures.

BARRIERS FOR LEADERS BEYOND THE RATIONAL

Why is it that despite these clear and known benefits to gender balance that many organizations are still hesitant to implement these changes?

These barriers arise from several common but unspoken fears from leaders. Feedback tells me no-one is calling these out. Without recognising these are real concerns and sharing how visionary leaders are boldly tackling these, progress of organisations and individuals will not be made.

Here are the 6 most common fears of current leaders:

Meetings: "My leadership team is difficult enough to manage, with different egos, ambitions, inability to share concerns in case of perceived weakness... adding in an unknown quantity of a female will create chaos/ risk loss of control (and I cannot tackle these in my usual man to man way or places)"

Emotions: "I do not know how or want to deal with a person who cannot take criticism, face tough challenge, respond to setbacks or have issues outside work being brought into work."

What ifs: "Managing the hassle for projects, for clients, for replacement and handovers when a female takes maternity leave, and additionally the unknown void if she is to return. Accommodating part time or flexible working arrangements and the additional responsibilities means her mind will no longer be 100% on the job."

Flexibility: "It is critical that tasks are completed on time and to the highest standard. Also it is essential that clients can always reach the person they require and teams can access individuals to progress actions and decisions at pace. This is a major risk if I must offer a female flexible working arrangements and even more in circumstances when a person needs to unexpectedly look after a sick child or relative."

"In accommodating flexible working, I risk ending up with so many people working different part time hours that it becomes incredibly difficult to manage holiday cover and workflow for the organisation."

Am I a bad person: "If I raise the issue of diversity and our need to improve, this implies we are not equitable now – I will therefore be labelled as sexist and I, my department and company will be perceived negatively."

Possible Traits: "I value those I work with, but knowing the demands at the highest level, I believe women do not have the stamina for long hours when a project deadline is required, the mental toughness in a crisis or ongoing hard knocks. They will not be taken seriously by colleagues due to lack of ferocity or presence, lacking commitment to make unpopular decisions. They juggle too many balls and cannot focus or as an opposite cannot control the degree of ferocity and directness which is uncomfortable for colleagues."

How does an individual or company overcome those barriers?

The following sections address these concerns directly:

ACTIONS BY VISIONARY LEADERS

Meetings: Not many CEOs voice their common struggle in leading a team of highly competent but all male, ambitious people who think alike but play political games to advance their own success and agendas, fearing openness as a sign of weakness that will be exploited by others. Feedback suggests these boards are far more fragile than one would assume from the outside, indeed some are even dysfunctional. Highly effective teams are those with high degree of trust and collaboration, who share commitments to advance the organisation first, are willing to share their concerns, make requests, meet promises, build with ideas to support a colleague's success, are aligned to decisions made in the boardroom and consistent in conversations inside and outside with all people. Successful leaders set out their expectations of their team, both collectively and individually, raising the bar, understanding concerns, positively and consistently enforcing it when new behaviours (or old behaviours) come forward in the meeting room.

Great leaders today are not expected to have all the answers but instead be good at asking insightful and probing questions whilst seeking suggestions from others. The introduction of any new member of the Board (male or female, internal or external appointment) causes change as positions are assessed and reset, so this is a great opportunity for leaders to refresh everyone as to their vision, expectations, ways of working, share purposes both for the organization and individuals, then structure agendas and separate conversations to enable dialogue to cover all elements that move situations forward (People, Possibilities, Plans, Performance & Produced actions).

Emotions: CEOs should allow themselves the luxury of continuous development. So many Boards struggle especially when asking for change by the rest of the organisation, when the employees will tell you, it is the management team that are the dinosaurs. A culture of ongoing personal and team development including the top is something that differentiates the Great from the average. Great CEOs encourage this ongoing learning – both individually and collectively.

Understanding and influencing people is one of the skills that creates unprecedented success and is never complete. Understanding people and what makes them fly, what makes them struggle, how they inter-relate, how to lead them, when knowing that there are so many different types of people, is invaluable.

Women fall into a range of types too. The women who have shown themselves to be high performers are the ones leaders want to have playing key roles in the company if they wish the organization to be sustainable.

Using the people techniques available through the many great training companies, it is very rewarding to have the skills to unlock what makes people tick, manage previous avoided conversations in a non-confrontational way and to see people transform and develop the areas they need to strengthen. I'd recommend www.paracomm.com, www.h2h.uk.com, as well as myself at www.realisepossibilities.com and www.boardroomreadywomen.com

Let me be clear – there are plenty of very talented women who possess all the demanded skills to lead and create unprecedented success, engaging colleagues and workforce as they do it. It is a talented CEO who can uncover and sponsor such women.

What ifs: Career planning, life planning are good conversations to have with line managers ongoing at quarterly reviews. When this is done, few surprises arise and company and employees can plan and accommodate changes in a mutual way for things such as succession planning and handovers. Equally, contact days when on maternity leave are beneficial. Like with flexibility, two way solutions can be found when planning a return. Returnies to work are often better than new recruits – as they already know the company, the systems and the people.

Flexibility: Flexibility is fast becoming a demand of the next generation, male and female, whose attitude to work and life balance is very different to the standard mindset we are familiar with. Therefore approaching this in a way that brings advantage to your company, attracting the best talent whilst ensuring the business needs are fully met, is a lever visionary leaders are keen to embed.

The basis is to have Flexibility as a two-way thing – enabling the company and individual needs to both be met. Seek mutual solutions to achieve business outcomes (the what) as opposed to being limited by traditional ways of working (the how). Have a method where the individuals suggest specific flexible working ways to meet their needs whilst making sure that company concerns and needed solutions are found together with a shared commitment to making it win win. There are lots of suggestions in HR guidelines that shape mutually reasonable conversations. This department is also useful to maintain an overview of all the flexible working so the collective solutions also stay workable.

Evidence shows that when flexibility is offered, alongside mutually agreed conditions, the organization and leader gain 120% of that individual's loyalty to deliver and excel for them, especially when it matters. Better still, it creates a culture where all individuals feel valued and this builds to the strongest team commitment and outputs.

Am I a bad person: Voicing what you stand for, as a future vision, is evidence of a strong leader, a driver of positive change. It is important to state that any current situation is not WRONG or Bad but what's MISSING is an opportunity to leverage how better gender balance can bring the organisation improved results.

Be ahead of the curve as at the time of writing, new UK/EU legislation is requiring organisations with more than 250 employees to publish their pay & bonus gaps between gender. This public information will prompt fresh assessments of company image and their leaders. As a global issue, the pressure from customers, clients, shareholders and future talent will build and build.

Possible Traits: Irrespective of gender, people must demonstrate they are leaders first, although beware reinforcing the dated traits of Command and Control as the organization will not be resilient to change and will become a dinosaur whatever the gender balance. Women may naturally show some skills which the organization needs, whilst not show some of these additionally desired traits. All this can be quickly and easily trained. Upon being made aware and experimenting with them in a development workshop, leaders will know if they can leverage them like many other skills.

Remember the objective of gender balance is that a blend of skills from men and women are brought to each leadership and management team, to create better thinking and better decisions.

It's an Individual leader's journey first, followed by the organisation's journey to success that leads to the culture changes required for gender balance. This culture shift involves moving from group think to broad think, going from the invisibility of talent to talent fully leveraged, limiting attitudes and behaviour to enabling attitudes and behaviour and going from circular conversations to transformation conversations.

These barriers begin as conscious bias – "I don't value women in the workplace", "I am not going to accommodate and I shall make decisions that discourage" (eg. starting a meeting at 6am to "prove" business is no place for the working mother!).

As the culture matures they shift to unconscious bias – all the barriers and probably more, that I listed as common but unspoken fears (evidenced by women retention at the middle to higher levels being low).

With a leadership mindset to change and actions applied, as I've highlighted here, the culture changes to conscious inclusion and with enough consistent reinforcement, you will naturally move on to world class, unconscious inclusion.

This will stand you head and shoulders above your competitors, your employees will be your ambassadors and together with stronger, agile performance you will attract your chosen clients, shareholder investors and have the pick of future talent. All building a sustainable future.

THE WATCH OUTS

It is important to also know what not to do.

These are based on my observations but not all people are in agreement.

Do not have **quotas**.

Always fill positions based on merit; Quotas have unintended consequences including undermining existing talent in leadership roles.

I see several companies set a % target but NOT time bound. The organisation does everything it can to balance the genders at all levels. KPIs measure progress to balance.

Actions include, advertising posts where females will most likely access them not just the usual trade journal. When vacancies arise, CVs may be assessed blind. The recruiting manager must write to the Board indicating if and why they've chosen a male candidate over a female one. There is visibility as to each department's gender balance, at all levels and pay gap differences. No-one wants to be bottom of the league table. It equally ensures the balance is not out of kilter the other way around – too many females is not good business either.

Do not avoid **conversations about gender.**

Making assumptions about what high potential women do and don't want without discussing with them, is foolhardy; Having honest conversations to explore future plans and find flexible solutions so no compromise in delivery of critical outcomes or client support is ideal. These should be with all employees, all genders and life stage. You can read the details on planning for these conversations in my book Boardroom Ready Women.

Raising the topic with an incumbent Board and creating the vision for change maybe where you need to start.

Do not **dismiss comments.**

Purporting to listen but dismissing concerns over colleague comments or behaviours, head in sand rather than dealing with grievances, leads to poor corporate culture and an undercurrent of mistrust and no loyalty. Beware of having a written policy that is not enforced. I see far too many Diversity and Inclusion statements in company's annual reports or on their websites alongside the overused phrase "people are our most important asset". However the % gender profile rarely matches the polished words.

Walk it, don't just talk it.

It is always powerful to ensure that concerns both from men and women are acted on and used as opportunities to reinforce the desired culture.

Do not leave Gender Balance to be the **responsibility only of the HR department.**

This is everyone's responsibility and a leader's accountability. Of-course use the skills and resources of this specialist function to co-ordinate the many elements required to create this culture change but delegating the outcome to one department and a Chief HR Officer, is doomed to fail.

STEPPING FORWARD

How can your desired cultural shift get started?

It is best to engage a few trusted advocates to steer the process.

Make stated the intent to leverage the advantage of gender balance.

Ask the right questions to establish where you are and collectively shape where you want to be (not quotas but targets without a time limit).

Then identify high performers and high potentials from talent reviews.

Initiate a programme of tailor made development support for these identified females and to educate and engage your mixed gender leadership teams. Combine this with your mainstream people insight support from HR. Highly recommended of-course is my proven successful workshop programme from www.RealisePossibilities.com or www.BoardroomReadyWomen.com.

In parallel, review or create policies and procedures and engage all leadership groups.

Seek out and recognise effective behaviours and outcomes that drive change especially in performance reviews, succession planning and recruitment.

Finally secure ongoing feedback from the women, the men and the leaders about what to Keep doing, Start doing, Do differently and Stop doing.

The final thing I should say, is whilst there are a lot of unconscious biases and barriers that boardrooms might have today, particularly if they are quite male orientated, don't let the culture change of an organisation have to be complete before seeing the appointment or promotion of a high potential woman. In my experience and feedback from the workshops I've run, 80% of the solution lies within action that can be taken by an individual.

Women can even be holding themselves back, but with this practical and effective C.A.R.B.O.N. Model toolkit, immediate awareness and change can be seen, benefiting the individual woman and the business area they work in, immediately. They can start overcoming their immediate barriers. Really, there is nothing stopping anyone.

If we encourage all leaders to understand the root cause of challenges in diversity and inclusion, introduce the application of practical solutions that enables them to establish gender balance in their workplace, they will see the benefits and fast.

All businesses, governments and people are talking about this but are hitting barriers and not succeeding in overcoming them. This is because they offer rational solutions to unconscious emotional barriers. I am trying to change the dialogue. My motivation is driven by a desire for better business performance, improved economic success and to see a balance with women also reaching positions of greater influence thereby creating more opportunities to improve their social environment & encourage the next generation.

Simple smart business sense.

Every individual woman who becomes familiar with the C.A.R.B.O.N. Way to Transform to Sparkling Success© will recognise the barriers they face in the corporate world and now have a practical way to address these barriers, enabling them to move forward and be a catalyst for their success and their organisation.

Not everyone wants to be or is capable of being a leader and that's OK. For those that do (especially women), we need encouragement and techniques to unlock their natural talent and also overcome barriers they face. I do not believe there needs to be a choice to sacrifice home life or career, as you can love and succeed with both if you create clarity, efficiency, priorities, self belief, belief in others and have great tools to assist you.

I believe, and have seen it and done it myself, that there are actions that you can take at every level in an organisation, to become a better leader, and become boardroom ready. Boardroom ready does not mean every woman should be or will be a Director or a Partner in a business, or that they even want to be, but embracing these practices will also enable individuals to perform better in their current role. It will create more enjoyment in the workplace, more fun and balance with loved ones, and generally an ability to live life to the full.

Whether you are that woman, that visionary leader or HR catalyst, you can make a difference in this, one of the most important of business topics today.

Branding Small Business

RAYMOND AARON

Branding is an incredibly important tool for creating and building your business. Large companies have been benefiting from branding ever since people first started selling things to other people. Branding made those businesses big.

If you're a small business owner, you probably imagine that small companies are different and don't need branding as much as large companies do. Not true. The truth is small businesses need branding just as much, if not more, than large companies.

Perhaps you've thought about branding, but assumed you'd need millions of dollars to do it properly, or that branding is just the same thing as marketing. Nothing could be further from the truth.

Marketing is the engine of your company's success. Branding is the fuel in that engine.

In the old days, salespeople were a big part of the selling process. They recommended one product over another and laid out the reasons why it was better. Salespeople had credibility because they knew about all the products, and customers often took the advice they had to offer.

Today, consumers control the buying process. They shop in big box stores, super-sized supermarkets, and over the Internet — where there are no salespeople. Buyers now get online and gather information beforehand. They learn about all the products available and look to see if there really is any difference between them. Consumers also read reviews and check social media to see if both the company and the product are reputable. In other words, they want to know what the brand is all about.

The way of commerce used to be: "Nothing happens till something is sold." Today it's: "Nothing happens till something is branded!"

DEFINING A BRAND

A brand is a proper name that stands for something. It lives in the consumer's mind, has positive or negative characteristics, and invokes a feeling or an image. In short, it's a person's perception of a product or a company.

When all goes well, consumers associate the same characteristics with a brand that the company talks about in its advertising, public relations, marketing and sales materials. Of course, when a product doesn't live up to what the company says about it, the brand gets a bad reputation. On the other hand, if a product or service over-delivers on the promises made, the brand can become a superstar.

RECOGNIZING BRANDING AND ITS CHARACTERISTICS

Branding is the science and art of making something that isn't unique, unique. Branding in the marketplace is the same as branding on a ranch. On a ranch, ranchers use branding to differentiate their cattle from every other rancher's cattle (because all cattle look pretty much the same). In the marketplace, branding is what makes a product stand out in a crowd of similar products. The right branding gets you noticed, remembered and sold — or perhaps I should say bought, because today it is all about buying, not selling.

There are four main characteristics of branding that make it an integral part of the marketing and purchasing process.

1. Branding makes you trustworthy and known

Branding makes a product more special than other products. With branding, a normal, everyday product has a personality, and a first and last name, and people know who you are.

In today's marketplace, most products are, more or less, just like their competition. Toilet paper is toilet paper, milk is milk, and a grocery store by any other name is still a grocery store. However, branding takes a product and makes it unique. For example, high-quality drinking water is available from just about every tap in the Western world and it's free, but people pay good money for it when it comes in a bottle. Branding takes bottled water and makes Evian.

Furthermore, every aspect of your brand gives potential customers a feeling or comfort level that they associate with you. The more powerful and positive that feeling is, the more easily and more frequently they will want to do business with you and, indeed, will do business with you.

2. Branding differentiates you from others

Strong branding makes you better than your competition, and makes your product name memorable and easy to remember. Even if your product is absolutely the same as every other product like it, branding makes it special. Branding makes it the first product a consumer thinks about when deciding to make a purchase.

Branding also makes a product seem popular. Everyone knows about it, which implicitly says people like it. And, if people like it, it must be good.

3. Branding makes you worth more money

The stronger your branding is, the more likely people are willing to spend that little bit extra because they believe you, your product, your service, or your business are worth it. They may say they won't, but they will. They do it all the time.

For example, a one-pound box of Godiva chocolates costs about $40; the same weight of Hershey's Kisses costs about $4. The quality of the chocolate isn't ten times greater. The reason people buy Godiva is that the brand Godiva means "gift" whereas the brand Hershey means "snack". Gifts obviously cost more than snacks.

4. Branding pre-sells your product

In the buying age, people most often make the decision on which products to pick up before they walk into the store. The stronger the branding, the more likely people are to think in terms of your product rather than the product category. For example, people are as likely, maybe even more likely, to add Hellmann's to the shopping list as they are to write down simply mayo. The same is true for soda, ketchup, and many other products with successful, strong branding.

Plus, as soon as a shopper gets to the shelf, branding can provide a quick reminder of what products to grab in a few ways:

- An icon or logo
- A specific color
- An audio icon

BRANDING IN A SMALL BUSINESS

Big companies spend millions of dollars on advertising, marketing, and public relations (PR) to build recognition of a new product name. They get their selling messages out to the public using television, radio, magazines, and the Internet. They can even throw money at damage control when necessary. The strategies for branding are the same in a small business, but the scale, costs, and a few of the tactics change.

Make your brand name work harder

The name of a small business can mean everything in terms of branding. Your brand name needs to work harder for your business than you do. It's the first thing a prospective customer sees, and it is how they will remember you. A brand name has to be memorable when spoken, and focused in its meaning. If the name doesn't represent what consumers believe about a product and the company that makes it, then that brand will fail.

In building your product's reputation and image, less is often significantly more. Make sure the name you choose immediately gives a sense of what you do.

Large corporations have millions of dollars to take a meaningless brand name and make it stand for something. Small businesses don't, so use words that really mean something. Strive for something interesting and be right on point. You don't need to be boring.

Plumbers, for example, would do well setting themselves apart with names like "The On-Time Plumber" or "24/7 Plumbing". The same is true for electricians, IT providers, or even marketing consultants. Plenty of other types of business are so general in nature they just don't work hard enough in a business or product name.

Even the playing field: The Net

The Internet has leveled the playing field for small businesses like nothing else. You can use the Internet in several ways to market your brand:

Website: Developing and maintaining a website is easier than ever. Anyone can find your business regardless of its size.

Social Media: Facebook and Twitter can promote your brand in a cost-effective manner.

BUILDING YOUR BRAND WITH THE BRANDING LADDER

Even if you do everything perfectly the first time (and I don't know anyone who does), branding takes time. How much time isn't just up to you, but you can speed things along by understanding the different levels of branding, as well as the business and marketing strategies that can get you to the top.

Introducing the Branding Ladder

Moving through the levels of branding is like climbing a ladder to the top of the marketplace. The Branding Ladder has five distinct rungs and, unlike stairs, you can't take them two at a time. You have to take them in order, and some businesses spend more time on each rung than others.

You can also think of the Branding Ladder in terms of a scale from zero to ten. Everyone starts at zero. If you properly climb the ladder, you can end up at 12 out of 10. The Branding Ladder below shows a special rung at the top of the ladder that can take your business over the top. The following section explains the Branding Ladder and how your small business can move up it.

THE BRANDING LADDER	
Brand Advocacy	12/10
Brand Insistence	10/10
Brand Preference	3/10
Brand Awareness	1/10
Brand Absence	0/10

Rung 1: Living in the void

Your business, in fact every business, starts at the bottom rung, which is called brand absence, meaning you have no brand whatsoever except your own name. On a scale of one to ten, brand absence is, of course, zero. That's the worst place to live and obviously the most difficult entrepreneurially. The good news is that the only way is up.

Ninety-seven percent of businesses live on this rung of the Branding Ladder. They earn far less than they want to earn, far less than they should earn, and far less than they would earn if they did exactly the same work under a real brand.

Rung 2: Achieving awareness

Brand awareness is a good first step up the ladder to the second rung. Actually, it's really good, especially because 97 percent of businesses never get there. You want people to be aware of you. When person A speaks to person B and says, "Have you heard of "The 24/7 Plumber?" You want the answer to be "yes".

On that scale of one to ten, however, brand awareness is only a one. It's better than nothing, but not that much better. Although people know of your brand, being aware doesn't mean that they are interested in buying it. Coca Cola drinkers know about Pepsi, but they don't drink it.

Rung 3: Becoming the preferred brand

Getting to the third rung, brand preference, is definitely a real step up. This rung means that people prefer to use your product or service rather than that of your competition. They believe there is a real difference between you and others, and you're their first choice. This rung is a crucial branding stage for parity products, such as bottled water and breakfast cereals, not to mention plumbers, electricians, lawyers, and all the others. Brand preference is clearly better than brand awareness, but it's less than halfway up the ladder.

Car rental companies represent a perfect example of why brand preference may not be enough. When someone lands at an airport and needs to rent a car on the spot, he or she may go straight to the preferred rental counter. If that company has a car available, it's a sale. However, if all the cars for that company have been rented, the person will move to the next rental kiosk without much thought, because one rental car is just as good as another.

Exerting Brand Preference needs to be easy and convenient

If all you have is brand preference, your business is on shaky ground and you can lose business for the feeblest of reasons. Very few people go to a second or third supermarket just to find their favorite brand of bottled water. Similarly, a shopper may prefer one store over another but, if both stores sell the same products, he or she will often go to the closest store even if it is not the better liked one. The reason for staying nearby does not need to be a dramatic one — the shopper may simply be tired, on a tight schedule, or not in the mood to travel.

Rung 4: Making it you and only you

When your customers are so committed to your product or service that they won't accept a substitute, you have reached the fourth rung of the Branding Ladder. All companies strive to reach this place, called brand insistence.

Brand insistence means that someone's experience with a product in terms of performance, durability, customer service, and image has been sufficiently exceptional. As a result, the product has earned an incredible level of loyalty.

If the product isn't available where the customer is, he or she will literally not buy something else. Rather, the person will look for the preferred product elsewhere. Can you imagine what a fabulous place this is for a company to be? Brand insistence is the best of the best, the perfect ten out of ten, the whole ball of wax.

Apple is a perfect example of brand insistence

Apple users don't just think, they know in their heads and hearts, that anything made by Apple is technologically-advanced, user-friendly, and just all-around superior. Committed to everything Apple, Mac users won't even entertain the thought that a PC may have positive attributes.

Apple people love everything about their Macs, iPads, iPhones, the Mac stores and all those apps. When the company introduces a new product, many of its brand-insistent fans actually wait in line overnight to be one of the first to have it. Steve Jobs is one of their idols.

Considering one big potential problem

Unfortunately, you can lose brand insistence much more quickly than you can achieve it. Brand-insistent customers have such high expectations that they can be disillusioned or disappointed by just one bad product experience. You also have to consistently reinforce the positives because insistence can fade over time. Even someone who has bought and re-bought a specific brand of car for the last 20 years can decide it's just time for a change. That's how fickle the world is.

At ten out of ten, brand insistence may seem like the top rung of the ladder, but it's not. One rung is actually better, and it involves getting your brand-insistent customers to keep polishing your brand for you.

Rung 5: Getting customers to do the work for you

Brand advocacy is the highest rung on the ladder. It's better than ten out of ten because you have customers who are so happy with your product that they want everyone to know about it and use it. Think of them as uber-fans. Not only do they recommend you to friends and family, they also practically shout your praises from the rooftops, interrupt conversations among strangers to give their opinion, and tell everyone they meet how fantastic you are. Most companies can only aspire to this level of customer satisfaction. Apple is one of the few large corporations in recent history that has brand advocates all over the world.

- Brand advocacy does the following five extraordinary things for your company. Brand advocacy:

- Provides a level of visibility that you couldn't pay for if you tried. Brand advocates are so enthusiastic they talk about you all the time, and reach people in ways general media and public relations can't. You get great visibility because they make sure people actually listen.

- Delivers free advertising and public relations. Companies love the extra super-positive messaging, all for free.

- Affords a level of credibility that literally can't be bought. Brand advocates are more than just walking testimonials. They are living proof that you are the best.

- Provides pre-sold prospective customers. Advocate recommendations carry so much weight that they are worth much more than plain referrals. They deliver customers ready and committed to purchasing your product or service.

- Increases profits exponentially. Brand advocates are money-making machines for your business because they increase sales and decrease marketing costs.

For these reasons, brand advocacy is 12 out of 10!!

BRANDING YOURSELF: HOW TO DO SO IN FOUR EASY WAYS

If you're interested in branding your product or company, you may not be sure where to begin. The good news: I'm here to help. You can brand in many ways, but here I pare it down to four ways to help you start:

Branding by association

This way involves hanging out with and being seen with people who are very much higher than you in your particular niche.

Branding by achievement

This way repurposes your previous achievements.

Branding by testimonial

This way makes use of the testimonials that you receive but have likely never used.

Branding by WOW

A WOW is the pleasantly unexpected, the equivalent of going the extra mile. The easiest and most certain way to WOW people is to tell them that you've written a book. To discover how you can write a book of your own, go to www.BrandingSmallBusinessForDummies.com.

Happiness: How to Experience the "Real Deals"

MARCI SHIMOFF

I was 41 years old, stretched out on a lounge chair by my pool and reflecting on my life. I had achieved all that I thought I needed to be happy.

You see, when I was a child, I thought there would be five main things that would ensure that I'd be happy: a successful career helping people, a loving husband, a comfortable home, a great body, and a wonderful circle of friends. After years of study, hard work, and a few "lucky breaks," I finally had them all. (Okay, so my body didn't quite look like Halle Berry's—but four out of five isn't bad!) You think I'd have been on the top of the world.

But surprisingly I wasn't. I felt an emptiness inside that the outer successes of life couldn't fill. I was also afraid that if I lost any of those things, I might be miserable. Sadly, I knew I wasn't alone in feeling this way.

While happiness is the one thing we all truly want, so few people really experience the deep and lasting fulfillment that fills our soul. Why aren't we finding it?

Because, in the words of the old country western song, we're looking for happiness in "all the wrong places."

Looking around, I saw that the happiest people I knew weren't the most successful and famous. Some were married, some were single. Some had lots of money, and some didn't have a dime. Some of them even had health challenges. From where I stood, there seemed to be no rhyme or reason to what made people happy. The obvious question became: *Could a person actually be happy for no reason?*

I had to find out.

So I threw myself into the study of happiness. I interviewed scores of scientists, as well as 100 unconditionally happy people. (I call them the Happy 100.) I delved into the research from the burgeoning field of positive psychology, the study of the positive traits that enable people to enjoy meaningful, fulfilling, and happy lives.

What I found changed my life. To share this knowledge with others, I wrote a book called *Happy for No Reason: 7 Steps to Being Happy from the Inside Out*.

One day, as I sat down to compile my findings, all the pieces of the puzzle fell into place. I had a simple, but profound "a-ha"—there's a continuum of happiness:

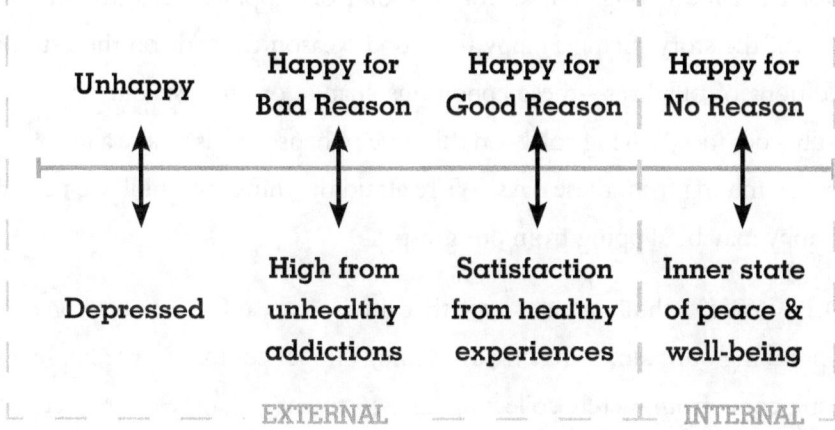

Unhappy: We all know what this means: life seems flat. Some of the signs are anxiety, fatigue, feeling blue or low—your "garden-variety" unhappiness. This isn't the same as clinical depression, which is characterized by deep despair and hopelessness that dramatically interferes with your ability to live a normal life, and for which professional help is absolutely necessary.

Happy for Bad Reason: When people are unhappy, they often try to make themselves feel better by indulging in addictions or behaviors that may feel good in the moment but are ultimately detrimental. They seek the highs that come from drugs, alcohol, excessive sex, "retail therapy," compulsive gambling, over-eating, and too much television-watching, to name a few. This kind of "happiness" is hardly happiness at all. It is only a temporary way to numb or escape our unhappiness through fleeting experiences of pleasure.

Happy for Good Reason: This is what people usually mean by happiness: having good relationships with our family and friends, success in our careers, financial security, a nice house or car, or using our talents and strengths well. It's the pleasure we derive from having the healthy things in our lives that we want.

Don't get me wrong. I'm all for this kind of happiness! It's just that it's only half the story. Being Happy for Good Reason depends on the external conditions of our lives—these conditions change or are lost, our happiness usually goes too. Relying solely on this type of happiness is where a lot of our fear is stemming from these days. We're afraid the things we think we need to be happy may be slipping from our grasp.

Deep inside, I think we all know that life isn't meant to be about getting by, numbing our pain, or having everything "under control." True happiness doesn't come from merely collecting an assortment of happy experiences. At our core, we know there's something more than this.

There is. It's the next level on the happiness continuum—Happy for No Reason.

Happy for No Reason: This is true happiness—a state of peace and well-being that isn't dependent on external circumstances.

Happy for No Reason isn't elation, euphoria, mood spikes, or peak experiences that don't last. It doesn't mean grinning like a fool 24/7 or experiencing a superficial high. Happy for No Reason isn't an emotion. In fact, when you are Happy for No Reason, you can have *any* emotion—including sadness, fear, anger or hurt—but you still experience that underlying state of peace and well-being.

When you're Happy for No Reason, you *bring* happiness to your outer experiences rather than trying to *extract* happiness from them. You don't need to manipulate the world around you to try to make yourself happy. You live from happiness, rather than *for* happiness.

This is a revolutionary concept. Most of us focus on being Happy for Good Reason, stringing together as many happy experiences as we can, like beads in a necklace, to create a happy life. We have to spend a lot of time and energy trying to find just the right beads so we can have a "happy necklace".

Being Happy for No Reason, in our necklace analogy, is like having a happy string. No matter what beads we put on our necklace—good, bad or indifferent—our inner experience, which is the string that runs through them all, is happy, and creates a happy life.

Happy for No Reason is a state that's been spoken of in virtually all spiritual and religious traditions throughout history. The concept is universal. In Buddhism, it is called causeless joy; in Christianity, the kingdom of Heaven within; and in Judaism it is called *ashrei*, an inner sense of holiness and health. In Islam it is called *falah*, happiness and well-being; and in Hinduism it is called *ananda*, or pure bliss. Some traditions refer to it as an enlightened or awakened state.

So how can you be Happy for No Reason?

Science is verifying the way. Researchers in the field of positive psychology have found that we each have a "happiness set-point," that determines our level of happiness. No matter what happens, whether it's something as exhilarating as winning the lottery or as challenging as a horrible accident, most people eventually return to their original happiness level. Like your weight set-point, which keeps the scale hovering around the same number, your happiness set-point will remain the same **unless you make a concerted effort to change it.** In the same way you'd crank up the thermostat to get comfortable on a chilly day, you actually have the power to reprogram your happiness set-point to a higher level of peace and well-being. The secret lies in practicing the habits of happiness.

Some books and programs will tell you that you can simply decide to be happy. They say just make up your mind to be happy—and you will be.

I don't agree.

You can't just decide to be happy, any more than you can decide to be fit or to be a great piano virtuoso and expect instant mastery. You can, however, decide to take the necessary steps, like exercising or taking piano lessons—and by practicing those skills, you can get in shape or give recitals. In the same way, you can become Happy for No Reason through practicing the habits of happy people.

All of your habitual thoughts and behaviors in the past have created specific neural pathways in the wiring in your brain, like grooves in a record. When we think or behave a certain way over and over, the neural pathway is strengthened and the groove becomes deeper—the way a well-traveled route through a field eventually becomes a clear-cut path. Unhappy people tend to have more negative neural pathways. This is why you can't just ignore the realities of your brain's wiring and *decide* to be happy! To raise your level of happiness, you have to create new grooves.

Scientists used to think that once a person reached adulthood, the brain was fairly well "set in stone" and there wasn't much you could do to change it. But new research is revealing exciting information about the brain's neuroplasticity: when you think, feel and act in different ways, the brain changes and actually rewires itself. You aren't doomed to the same negative neural pathways for your whole life. Leading brain researcher Dr. Richard Davidson, of the University of Wisconsin says, "Based on what we know of the plasticity of the brain, we can think of things like happiness and compassion as skills that are no different from learning to play a musical instrument or tennis …. it is possible to train our brains to be happy."

While a few of the Happy 100 I interviewed were born happy, most of them learned to be happy by practicing habits that supported their happiness. That means wherever you are on the happiness continuum, it's entirely in your power to raise your happiness level.

In the course of my research, I uncovered 21 core happiness habits that anyone can use to become happier and stay that way. You can find all 21 happiness habits at www.HappyForNoReason.com

Here are a few tips to get you started:

1. **Incline Your Mind Toward Joy.** Have you noticed that your mind tends to register the negative events in your life more than the positive? If you get ten compliments in a day and one criticism, what do you remember? For most people, it's the criticism. Scientists call this our "negativity bias" — our primitive survival wiring that causes us to pay more attention to the negative than the positive. To reverse this bias, get into the daily habit of consciously registering the positive around you: the sun on your skin, the taste of a favorite food, a smile or kind word from a co-worker or friend. Once you notice something positive, take a moment to savor it deeply and feel it; make it more than just a mental observation. Spend 20 seconds soaking up the happiness you feel.

2. **Let Love Lead.** One way to power up your heart's flow is by sending loving kindness to your friends and family, as well as strangers you pass on the street. Next time you're waiting for the elevator at work, stuck in a line at the store or caught up in traffic, send a silent wish to the people you see for their happiness, well-being, and health. Simply wishing others well switches on the "pump" in your own heart that generates love and creates a strong current of happiness.

3. **Lighten Your Load.** To make a habit of letting go of worries and negative thoughts, start by letting go on the physical level. Cultural anthropologist Angeles Arrien recommends giving or throwing away 27 items a day for nine days. This deceptively simple practice will help you break attachments that no longer serve you.

4. **Make Your Cells Happy.** Your brain contains a veritable pharmacopeia of natural happiness-enhancing neurochemicals — endorphins, serotonin, oxytocin, and dopamine — just waiting to be released to every organ and cell in your body. The way that you eat, move, rest, and even your facial expression can shift the balance of your body's feel-good-chemicals, or "Joy Juice", in your favor. To dispense some extra Joy Juice — smile. Scientists have discovered that smiling decreases stress hormones and boosts happiness chemicals, which increase the body's T-cells, reduce pain, and enhance relaxation. You may not feel like it, but smiling — even artificially to begin with — starts the ball rolling and will turn into a real smile in short order.

5. **Hang with the Happy.** We catch the emotions of those around us just like we catch their colds — it's called emotional contagion. So it's important to make wise choices about the company you keep. Create appropriate boundaries with emotional bullies and "happiness vampires" who suck the life out of you. Develop your happiness "dream team" — a mastermind or support group you meet with regularly to keep you steady on the path of raising your happiness.

"Happily ever after" isn't just for fairytales or for only the lucky few. Imagine experiencing inner peace and well-being as the backdrop for everything else in your life. When you're Happy for No Reason, it's not that your life always looks perfect — it's that, however it looks, you'll still be happy!

By Marci Shimoff. Based on the New York Times bestseller *Happy for No Reason: 7 Steps to Being Happy from the Inside Out*, which offers a revolutionary approach to experiencing deep and lasting happiness. The woman's face of the *Chicken Soup for the Soul* series and a featured teacher in *The Secret*, Marci is an authority on success, happiness, and the law of attraction. To order *Happy for No Reason* and receive free bonus gifts, go to www.happyfornoreason.com/mybook.

Sex, Love and Relationships

DR. JOHN GRAY

Just as great sex is important to lasting love, good health is important to sex and relationships. About 12 years ago, I cured myself of early stage Parkinson's disease. The doctors were amazed, but my wife was even more amazed. She noted that our relationship and sex life had become dramatically better. It turns out that the natural supplements I used to reverse Parkinson's can also make you more attentive and loving in your relationship. At that point, I realized that good relationship skills alone were not enough to sustain love and passion for a lifetime.

I shared many insights gained from my 40 years' experience as a marriage counselor and coach in *Men Are From Mars, Women Are From Venus*. And while my insights go a long way towards helping men and women understand and support each other, good communication skills alone are not always enough. For better relationships, we not only need to be healthy, but we must also experience optimum brain function.

If you are tired, depressed, anxious, not sleeping well, or in pain, then certainly romantic feelings will become a thing of the past. My recovery from Parkinson's revealed to me the profound connection between the quality of our health and our relationships. This insight has motivated me, over the past twelve years, to research the secrets of optimum health as a foundation for lasting love.

These are health secrets that are generally not explored in medical school. In medical school, doctors are indoctrinated into the culture of examining the symptoms, identifying the sickness, and prescribing a drug to treat that sickness. They learn very little about how to be healthy or to sustain successful relationships.

There are no university courses entitled "Better Nutrition For Better Sex". Drugs sometimes save lives, but they also have negative side effects that do little to preserve the passion in a relationship. Ideally, drugs should be used as a last resort and 90 % of our health plan should be drug free. From this perspective, the heath care crisis, as well as our high rate of divorce in America, is indirectly caused by our dependence on doctors and prescription drugs.

Most people have not even considered that taking prescribed drugs (even for the small stuff) can weaken their relationships, which in turn makes them more vulnerable to more disease. For example, if you are feeling depressed or anxious, a drug may numb your pain, but it does nothing to help you correct the cause of your problem. It can even prevent you from feeling your natural motivation to get the emotional support you need. In a variety of ways, our common health complaints are all expressions of two major conditions: our lack of education to identify and support unmet gender-specific emotional needs; and our lack of education to identify and support unmet gender-specific nutritional needs.

With an understanding of natural solutions that have been around for thousands of years, drugs are not needed to treat many common complaints. Some symptoms like low energy, weight gain, allergies, hormonal imbalance, mood swings, poor sleep, indigestion, lack of focus, ADD and ADHD, procrastination, low motivation, memory loss, decreased libido, PMS, vaginal dryness, muscle and joint pain, or the lack of passion in life and/or our relationships can be treated drug-free. By using drugs (even over-the-counter drugs) to treat these common complaints, our bodies and relationships are weakened, making us more vulnerable to bigger and more costly health challenges like cancer, diabetes, heart disease, auto-immune disease, dementia, and Alzheimer's. In simple terms, by handling the easy stuff (the common complaints) without doctors and drugs, we can protect ourselves from the big stuff (cancer, heart disease, dementia, etc.) We can be healthy and also enjoy lasting love and passion in our personal lives.

Even if you are taking anti-depressants or hormone replacement therapy, sometimes all it takes to stop treating the symptom is to directly handle the cause. With specific mineral orotates (something most people have never heard of) or omega three oil from the brains of salmon, your stress levels immediately drop and you begin to feel happy and in love again.

For every health challenge, we have explored the effects on our relationships, with as well as natural remedies that can sometimes produce immediate positive results. You can find these natural solutions to common health complaints for free at my website: www.MarsVenus.com.

What they don't teach in medical school is how to be healthy and happy without the use of drugs or hormone replacement. By refusing drugs and taking responsibility for your health, a wealth of new possibilities can become available to you. We are designed to be healthy and happy, and it is within our reach if we commit to increasing our knowledge.

New research regarding the brain differences in men and women reveals how specific nutritional supplements, combined with gender-specific relationship and self-nurturing skills, can stimulate the hormones of health, happiness and increased energy. Over the past 10 years in my healing center in California, I witnessed how natural solutions coupled with gender-specific relationship skills could solve our common health complaints without drugs. By addressing these common complaints without prescribed drugs, not only do we feel better, but our relationships have the potential to improve dramatically.

Ultimately the cause of all our common complaints is higher stress levels. Researchers around the world all agree that chronic stress levels in our bodies provide a basis for any and all disease to take hold. An easy and quick solution for lowering our stress reactions is specific nutritional support combined with gender-smart relationship skills. Extra nutritional support is needed because stress depletes the body very quickly of essential nutrients. When a car engine is running more quickly, it uses fuel more quickly. When we are stressed, we need both extra nutrients and extra emotional support. Understanding what we need to take and where to get it requires education. Every week day at www.MarsVenus.com I have a live daily show where I freely answer questions and provide this much-needed new gender-specific insight.

At www.MarsVenus.com, we are happy to share what we have learned for creating healthy bodies and positive relationships. You can find a host of natural solutions for common complaints and feel confident that you have the power to feel fully alive with an abundance of energy and positive feelings that will enrich all your relationships.

Break Through Your Barriers & Live Your Dreams

Sandra Westland

Every woman deserves to feel powerful and successful, and the opportunity to do so stands right before her. She doesn't have to be a warrior to smite every dragon or burn down every obstacle that stands in her way. She simply needs to connect with and be her real, authentic self. So her journey to success begins by standing still, by being curious about the world of potential that exists within her and in front of her, and by understanding her inner world in order to ignite change in her outer one towards her success.

But, what stops her from becoming the author of her own life, from being all she can be? The glass ceiling, the unofficial barrier that prevents women from rising up to executive positions or from running their successful businesses, does still exist. Yet, in my twenty-five years of education, hypno-psychotherapy and peak performance training, I see, more significantly, an individual's own inner glass ceiling capping and limiting the success in life that is there for the taking.

To be a woman is to be extraordinary. We all have it within us to move beyond an ordinary life and its everyday limitations to embrace our desires and possibilities, harness our untold natural potential and live the life we are meant to live —a life of personal freedom in which we simply are our natural, awesome selves. Your power is switched on when you embrace, embody, express and enjoy being a woman. Your energy is released when you learn to live truly in your own skin. I love being a woman, and I love continuing to find out just what that is like for me.

This is a journey of discovering your place in life as a woman and as a woman in business, a voyage into your inner mind's processing and the terrain of your inner world, deeper than your conscious mind can be aware of. It is an expedition through self-alignment, forming the detail of your desired outcomes, shaping your life to fit with your passions, sourcing the energy that drives you, thus smashing your glass ceiling and allowing your transformation to unfold. Just as I experienced my own first steps, I want you also to stride out along this path and the journey of becoming your potential. The message I write within the pages of *Smashing Your Glass Ceiling* takes you through this fascinating journey where "Wow, I didn't realize that" and "No wonder I wasn't getting to where I wanted to" are familiar insights.

HOW DOES IT ALL WORK?

The tools you will need for such a journey of self-discovery are drawn from Neuro-Linguistic Programming (NLP), guided imagery, and a gentle questing into uncovering your own uniqueness and meaning in life. In blending these time-tested methods into one programme, it's possible to break through all that's holding you back in life.

From my own personal experience as a woman and as a psychotherapist and trainer, I've found that one of the most powerful tools we naturally have and need to embrace first is the power of imagination; even if you think you have one or not, you really do have an amazing, creative imagination. It just may need awakening and a little encouraging. I would love to show you just how powerful your imagination can be and how crucial it is to connect with you and be your own woman. In beginning this imaginative journey, you are sparking off a chain of events that produce fundamental changes in your physical body, starting with the neurological processes that will link to your biology and produce within you "decision states" leading to the different outcomes that you want, easily and naturally. Imagine the decisions that you can make or the actions that you can take when you are feeling confident, in balance and aligned to your vision, compared to the choices that you opt for when you are upset, anxious, depressed and out of sync with yourself.

By guiding your imagination, you can form an internal vision in which you are taking the right path for you to succeed in your life, and then formulate just what that is. As you immerse yourself in the excitement and the thrill of being on the right road to greatness, you tap into the inner confidence and self-reliance, inner freedom and success awareness that generate your momentum to smashing your glass ceiling. The power is always within you. It's just a case of summoning and connecting with it.

Imagine also gaining new understanding into how you process information from your "now" experiences, how you view the world, how you communicate with others and how they communicate with you. Imagine how much easier your life would be. You can learn how to recognize ways of processing external data and how, by modifying your communication in a way that makes sense to others, your relationships become infinitely warmer, richer and more connected.

Think about meeting me in the flesh for the first time, already knowing how my inner world works. Wouldn't it be good to know I'm an auditory person? Why? Well, my world is very much filtered through sounds. I will be finely tuned into noise … all noise. I will get distracted with too much of it, and I will recognize very slight changes in your voice, tone and pitch. So I will hear a hint of doubt or an emotion rising from within you just by hearing your voice. If you speak too slowly or very loudly, this will create a dissonance within me. If you use language that talks about "viewing something" or "seeing what you mean" or "having a handle on this or that" instead of "sounds like" or "listen to", I will feel a mismatch between us. Don't click your pen or tap it on the table if you want me to be relaxed! It's only a slight inner discomfort, but it undeniably shapes how I experience you and your communication. Upon our meeting, if you appreciate my world and I appreciate yours, we will hit it off with ease. I will look to communicate to you through your world, which may be visual, auditory, kinesthetic or auditory digital, all very different ways of experiencing and processing, and you can do the same for me.

GETTING TO KNOW YOUR GLASS CEILING

Your internal glass ceiling may have been created from prejudgments, prejudices, cultural and social attitudes that operate deep within the unconscious, taken in when young. So, it's crucial to find these out and know how they work for you, to understand the inner conflicts that are holding you back and what they mean. In speaking with a senior executive upon her reading *Smashing Your Glass Ceiling*, she'd suddenly become aware of how she was dressing like a man for her banking boardroom meetings. It wasn't her at all, but after further exploration, she realized she had unconsciously thought it would help men relate to her and allow her to be "taken seriously". She was shocked at how unconscious this had been, but she was relieved to learn it and is now enjoying the fun of finding out who she is as a woman in business and what clothes this exploration leads her to wearing. It is only by excavating these unconscious gender biases and other judgments that contribute towards making your own ceiling that you can reveal your real, natural self to yourself and the world. In understanding yourself more and knowing just who you are and how you are in the world, you become free to choose how to respond to situations and to people, and then you really begin to own your own life.

I am wondering just what you are thinking, having read these thousand plus words. Is this possible for you or is your glass ceiling giving you bother, preventing you from imagining and thinking of all that you can be? What does your ceiling hold and what is it whispering to you right now? What is your "default" setting?

Are you someone who assumes you won't find a car parking space and prove yourself right, or do you simply know that it doesn't matter where you park and thus usually find one just when and where you need it? Is a potential redundancy at work a chance to do something different, or a terrible catastrophe that you will never escape? Your attitudes play a massive part in your life experiences, and to how much you can grow. Zig Ziglar's famous saying "Your attitude determines your altitude" is so true. So, how do your attitudes determine how successful you can be?

I have lived and refined through my own personal journey a framework of all the things that are crucial to help you aspire to be. Let's make a start right now, something to get you thinking. Let's peek into those achieving just what you want and begin to emulate some of what they do and how they are. It's as good a place as any to start!

In NLP terms, this is called "modeling". In modeling the behaviors and habits of successful people, we're seeking to learn from successful businesswomen and successful women just what it is that they do, and what it is that they have that makes them successful; not to become them, but to incorporate their winning behaviours into our repertoire, choosing those which are congruent with us and amplifying them. I often explore other women that I admire and am drawn to. In carefully watching what they do and exploring this within my own life, in my way, I can open up to further resources that I naturally have, but have yet to connect with. In Sue Knight's' words, "If you spot it, you've got it." (NLP at Work, 2013)

Now to stoke up those neurological pathways as we vamp it up a little more and transport you forward into your own fabulous future. Familiarize yourself with the state of being successful with no glass ceiling, as if you've already accomplished that level of success, a dress rehearsal if you like. Put on the mantle of success and ask yourself how and what do you feel, how would your day evolve, what can you do now that you couldn't do before. How would others perceive you? Get your brain to make it a done deal so that it can look for it, search it out and create it. This is the self-fulfilling prophecy at its most positive, potent and powerful.

Anticipate now becoming friendly and familiar with a future you who has everything you need and want and to be able to use the guidance of that future you – the answers may very well surprise you. My future self enlightened me as to my fear of success! This helped me find my inner glass ceiling and the meaning of it all, so I could smash it and really begin to find out just what I could do and what was possible in life. I believe that to guide others you have to have lived the journey yourself, and so my own personal journey has and is this path too, encompassing where I am finding myself ... as a woman, an educator, therapist and businesswoman. This is a journey I don't ever intend to stop.

PEELING BACK THE ONION

There is so much more to explore! As humans, we've infinite depths, so exploring your inner beliefs, your values and mission is crucial for success. It's the peeling back of the onion, layer by layer (corny, I know), but I assure you that the exploration, while deep, is richly rewarding. Wouldn't you rather know what's holding you back and why you may feel frustrated with yourself? I know I would. I simply want to make the most of my time on this earth and experience it as much as possible. Life is to be lived and not simply endured and got through.

Excavate your inner beliefs, isolate the limiting ones that have held you back, and then you will easily and naturally begin to fly! Once figured out, you become empowered as you re-think and re-frame beliefs into being resourceful, productive and desirable, and turn them into second nature.

Let's go one deeper. Do you know just what it is that you value, all those things that are really important to you? Are they aligned with your life? These are your GPS, and if you're frustrated, feel trapped in the mundane of life or have unwanted physical/emotional symptoms, then value fine-tuning is needed for you to move forward in the direction that you want to go. Let's not be sidetracked by detours, road closures and an unclear destination. Being authentic and all that you need to know is what you value so that you're able to craft your mission for the ultimate alignment. In *Smashing Your Glass Ceiling* or my Success workshops, you will not short-change yourself here. I will journey with you, helping you along the way through a process of simple, yet profoundly powerful steps.

When you are fully aligned, there will be no holding you back. You'll meet the right person at the right time, and you'll have the right skills to achieve your goals. Everything will fall into place like a jigsaw puzzle, and you'll have "the strength, the patience, and the passion to reach for the stars", to borrow the words of a courageously inspiring woman, Harriet Tubman.

LOADING UP ON INTERNAL RESOURCES

It's not all plain sailing, and you *will* be derailed by the unexpected, but what makes someone a success is their ability to keep going, even when challenged. So, one of the final steps in the Programme is to load you up with the internal resources to get you through when things get sticky, and when, quite frankly, you wonder why you bother. NLP strategies reprogram how we react and respond to such times, making a monumental difference to how you experience your life. If you're feeling down on yourself, I will show you that you can change your physiology. If you're getting increasingly anxious about an upcoming meeting, you can change your self-talk, the inner conversation you're having with yourself, to something more upbeat, more encouraging and more positive.

Powerful NLP strategies are there for you to use at any time and in any situation. Your life will be richer and filled with more options when you are able to redirect your thinking and focus, stay resourceful in stressful situations, and generate behaviors and outcomes that are positive for you and your life.

Finally, if this chapter has inspired you to delve deeper into Smashing your Glass Ceiling, the book comes with a number of bonuses, some of which can be downloaded from my website, www.SmashingYourGlassCeiling.com for you to enjoy absolutely free. So, get started now and embrace the fact that you are an extraordinary woman.

TAKING THE FIRST STEP

All of us have to start somewhere. I did when I was thirty-four, when I found myself looking at twenty-six more years before retirement, counting the years and the days till the next school holiday. Not how I imagined my life would be.

By becoming curious, asking questions of myself and tapping into effective life-changing techniques that opened me up to the power and potential of the mind, I'm on a fascinating journey. I'm continuing to smash my own internal glass ceiling, and am living out my passion to enhance the lives of other women. I am certainly not "sorted out", nor have I "self-actualized" and not every day is "grrreat", but I know that every day is an adventure with the chance to grow further and find out more about just what is possible.

The more women I meet and work with, the more I learn and the more I gather evidence to support my belief that, as women, we owe it to ourselves to be extraordinary. This is my invitation to you to take the first steps with me on your own journey of becoming all you wish to be.

Sandra Westland is an experienced educator, therapist and successful businesswoman who helps others to find their passion and fulfil their dreams. She has a Master's degree in Existential Psychotherapy, an Education Honours degree, and is a practicing Advanced Hypnotherapist and NLP practitioner. Her doctoral thesis explores women and their relationship with their bodies. She is the author of Smash Your Glass Ceiling and co-author of Thinking Therapeutically.

Sandra is a Director of the Contemporary College of Therapeutic Studies, where she trains people at life changing junctures to be aspiring therapists, so they too can enjoy the enriching privilege of helping others to find their path in life. She is also a co-founder of Self Help School™, which provides psycho-education for the public and is an international speaker on the power of the mind for change.

Honor Your Inner Treasures

CELINA TIO

COLLECTIVE CREATED ME

"We are all created from our experiences, and the first step towards embracing our inner treasures is to acknowledge this. You are wonderful, and the experiences that took you to this point are all part of that. Do not be afraid of yourself; instead, let yourself shine." This quote is from my recent book, *Honor Your Inner Treasures*. It's an underlying principle of that work, and its message is most certainly applicable to what you're about to read in this chapter of *The Authorities*. Collective Created Me explains in the *Honor Your Inner Treasures* book, how most of our beliefs are obtained through training and repetition, and assumed personality through education. Becoming aware of the Collective Created Me is extremely beneficial because it puts you on the road to self-acceptance and realization, forgiveness, independence, appreciation and true happiness.

Think about this for a moment: do you remember someone in your family being sick when you were a child? Were the hours spent in family time talking about symptoms, where pain started, where it ended, how long it lasted, and medicines? It's likely that much of the conversation also revolved around nurses, doctors' assessments and trips to the hospital. Soon, with so much health and sickness related information taken in, you unconsciously started to become so familiar enough with that illness that you accepted it as just part of your family. It became so normal that you could quickly respond to questions about it as if it were your illness, too. "My uncle Charlie had it, and so did his son and my grandmother. It runs in our family."

Imagine if the conversation you heard about Uncle Charlie's illness had been about the way that healthy habits, physical activities, and letting go of toxic thoughts helped him recover. What would you have learned to do then in the event of an illness?

This example of negativity changing your perspective is applicable to other life experiences. What about love and relationships? Conversations about unfaithfulness, divorce, unhealthy relationships, abuse, violence? How has the negativity of those conversations affected your beliefs and the actions you've taken in life? Money is another example. People often say they never have enough money. Stories are shared about someone's new business failing, or friends who've lost their homes because they couldn't make their mortgage payments. Wouldn't stories of success have a more positive impact to encourage others to improve in their lives?

Most people receive diagnoses during their lives pertaining to health, personal finances, the country's economy, beauty, fashion and relationships. Usually, these diagnoses are fully accepted as truth and fact. There is an alternative, however. Why not see a diagnosis as feedback of that exact, precise moment and utilize it as the moment of opportunity to change, to create, to expand, to become, to discover, is opening up for you?

People often say when a door closes a window opens, and wait for the window to open right in front of them. Often, hoping that the window will magically pop open and the situation will change. The sad thing is, it may take a while and in the meantime the beliefs that life is not fair, life is hard or life is good to others start to run your thoughts.

I want you to know that all windows and doors are always open for you. Even more, there are no windows, there are no doors, because once you embrace your greatness you are free to live with purpose.

Going back to our example of listening to other people's life experiences, can you perceive how your fears and beliefs originated during these events? The occasions are wonderful moments to enjoy and remember the past, but sometimes people retell stories about illnesses with as much detail as they can recall. It's possible the now-adult children have no recollection of the event's seriousness because they remember with a child's naïveté only how happy they were about recovery. Now, listening to the story of an experience in your life that evoked sadness, these adults inevitably feel pulled down and relive that low-energy feeling. You can change that feeling in you and all the people around you. Next time you are at a reunion be sure to evoke moments that bring joy and laughter. Everyone will leave feeling great, having enjoyed the party, and with a more positive attitude for the next adventure in their life.

BECOME AWARE - CONNECT WITH YOUR INNER BEING

Let go of the stories and let go of others' experiences. Start living your own.

Embrace the belief that your life is complete and absolute just as is. Take a deep breath, aware of your body, starting at the top and working your way down. Begin with your scalp, your hair, your temples, your forehead, your eyebrows, your eyes, then move on until you reach the tip of your toes. It's important to take in every part of yourself so don't stop at the surface. Recognize your organs and their functions, even noting your breath as it travels into your lungs and fills you with pure oxygen. Become aware of your being. I ask that you become aware of your being, know that you look into the mirror or take a selfie and analyze it to see if you have wrinkles, or criticize your body shape. Stop judging yourself and start knowing yourself.

Selfies have become, to many, a tool to prove oneself, or a tool of confirmation of existence, presence and self-acceptance, and others' approval of the moment that is being lived.

As if the moment being lived needs external approval to be considered as a "perfect moment" and only then sharing it with the world.

When you look at the moment you are living as an image that "looks good" or "like happiness", the gap between what you are doing "looks great", and truly feeling great, is large. There is no enjoyment or happiness if it always depends on others' opinions. Making a picture look good when the emotions you are feeling at the moment don't match the illusion of the created image is keeping you from living a true honest happy moment.

Different from this is taking a picture to capture a moment of real pleasure and happiness, and the peace and joy that healthy relationships and celebrations bring. Those are photographs that recall true emotions of happiness, in turn aligning your whole being into feeling truly amazing. These selfies are not only a moment taken with a camera; they are taken into your soul, leaving a long-lasting impression in your life. Those are moments that you will truly love to share with others without deleting anything. What is your selfie telling you when you look at it? What is that image revealing?

Become aware of yourself and the moment without editing. Be completely honest about everything. In this moment of self-awareness, accept everything – your age, aches, sadness, longings, best memories, dreams – without shyness, even if they look too big at this moment. Become aware because for the first time in your life you will be truly, honestly and entirely present with yourself, as you know yourself to be at this moment. What is your inner self telling you? This is the true SELF you should be contemplating.

If you do this, for the first time in your life you will be truly, honestly and entirely present. Your unique, true self will be revealed. For many people, doing this will be the scariest meeting of their lives. To me it is the most amazing!

When working with my clients, this point of their journey is the most exciting to me. As their guide to reaching their true inner being throughout the Honor Your Inner Treasures™ Program, the transformation the client undergoes is magical, because their life suddenly expands as they embrace and accept fully their inner self.

YOUR EMOTIONS ARE POWERFUL. LEARN FROM THEM.

Pretending is the only sure thing someone does when they are denied their true feelings. Pretending to feel well, smiling just with the movement of the facial muscles, repeating clichés as a consolation to true feelings, and distancing ourselves from loved ones or hiding from life aren't effective measures. Not talking about problems doesn't solve them. On the contrary, the repetition of those actions and inner messages undoubtedly becomes the reality in your life, which extends the sadness, insecurity, lack of confidence, and low-energy life. It's an unhealthy cycle, difficult to break. Have you ever heard people complaining about the good luck of others, or blaming the sad circumstances in their life on other people's lives? If you come close to a person behaving this way, stay away. You don't want to adopt that attitude.

You can change, you can become more, and you can be the best amazing you because you truly, genuinely feel it. Sharing your life with others with honesty, because there is absolutely nothing to hide, is liberating. Accept that you are a human being experiencing life, and in the process are growing, becoming, expanding, and evolving.

Through this process there will be moments that call for change, whether of habits, beliefs, actions, or behaviors. Change is a process of evolving into a different state. The emotions that you carry through the transition are of most importance. Are you making the change out of resentment or fear? Is it happening because you don't feel you're enough? Or are you just resigning yourself because you are obedient to unhappiness. What if you make the change because you know that you would love and enjoy doing something different?

Ask yourself what you need to make this change? Maybe it's taking a course or learning something new. Going through training is a fun ride when all you are doing is acquiring new skills to master what you love to do! Don't let the fear of change keep you from becoming healthier and happier. You look and feel healthy and beautiful when you are enjoying the moments that you are creating in your life. Change gives you jolts of energy that propels you to do more.

CHANGE TO THE POSITIVE SIDE OF LIFE

"Change the thinking positive and acting negative attitude." – Celina Tio

I hear people talking about difficult situations in their lives that end with usual comments like "I'm staying positive," "I'm trying to think positive" or "Hopefully…" However, simply repeating the mantra "I'm staying positive" does not make it true. When you are vibrating in the true sense of positive energy your life has no room for negative energy. Positive will always see, hear, understand, interpret, and plan in a constructive manner. When clients come for their first consultations with me, I listen attentively to their voices. From their tones I can hear the negative energy of unhealed wounds, regardless of the words they use. They tell their stories as if they've become comfortable hurting. This is a common means of self-defense and emotional survival.

In their journeys through the Honor Your Inner Treasures™ Program, clients delve into their true selves and are guided through the process of transmuting their thoughts into a positive perspective. This transformation occurs once we do the necessary inner work at the soul level, which is the purest essence of being. Anger may become understanding and compassion; resentment an opportunity for self-reflection and inner growth; and solitude a time of self-forgiveness and self-acceptance. The more you discover about your inner being, the closer you are to the positive energy of your true self. Knowing that each step my clients take brings them closer to their inner being of positive creation gives me great joy. It is important to create life experiences in such a way that, when you reflect on the past, all you see is a magical garden of your own design that you can be proud of having imagined, lived, grown and created.

Let's do an exercise that will assist you with looking at decisions based on fear. You will need to sit comfortably on a chair and have with you a pad of paper and a pen. Imagine an "X" mark on the floor to your right that represents the change that you want to make, and an "X" to your left side. The "X" mark on the left side represents the negative reasons that you have to make the change in your life and the "X" on the right side represents positive ones.

On the paper write the reasons you want to make the change. For example, let's say that the decision you want to make is about a change in career. Write on the paper the thoughts that have crossed your mind. Use one piece of paper per thought about the issue. (It is important to follow these steps carefully.) Now, decide if the thought you've written is negative or positive and put the paper to your left or right side. Use the guide on page 9 to help you determine whether your thoughts are positive or negative.

THOUGHT	LEFT SIDE	RIGHT SIDE
<u>I'm so fed up with my job.</u> I think I'll look for another one.	X	
<u>My job is so boring.</u> After doing the same thing every day for so long, it is not *exciting* anymore.	X	
I have been thinking of working part-time so I can go back to school. I'll have to cut down on expenses but I know it will be ok because I have some savings.		X
I have a job offer in another company <u>but</u> I would have to take a few courses to meet their requirement. a) I don't have the money to pay for the training b) It's hard to go back to class c) All your other "BUTS"	X	
<u>I hate going to work. The place is so toxic. The gossiping and competition is just sickening.</u>	X	

As you can see, on the column for thoughts I have underlined the negative comments. On the fourth example the word but is underlined because the "buts" are so big in our lives. You truly have to listen closely when you speak. Until you change your internal dialogue and are able to do this spontaneously, it is best to do this exercise by writing it on pieces of paper. Doing this will change the thinking positive and acting negative attitude that most people have without realizing why their lives are so difficult. Once you have identified your thought process about the issue, you can transform it and move all your thoughts to the positive side.

THOUGHT	LEFT SIDE	TRANSFORM & MOVE TO THE RIGHT SIDE
I'm so fed up with my job. I think I'll look for another one.	X	I'm more than ready to expand my possibilities. I know I have learned enough in my current position so I now realize I have room to grow.
My job is so boring. After doing the same thing every day for so long, it is not *exciting* anymore.	X	I love the feeling of excitement that bring new possibilities and learning new things. Change is great because I'm now ready.
I have been thinking of working part-time so I can go back to school. I'll have to cut down on expenses and [but] I know it will be ok because I have some savings.		This example shows how something that could be big "<u>but</u> I don't have money" is removed as an inconvenience and seen as something to work through.
I have a job offer in another company <u>but</u> I would have to take a few courses to meet their requirement. a) I don't have the money to pay for the training b) It's hard to go back to class c) All your other "BUTS"	X	This example is the opposite of the one above. Listen to all of your buts because they only pave the road ahead with more of the same in your life today. "No money" only brings you no money.
I hate going to work. The place is so toxic. The gossiping and competition is just sickening.	X	I have changed. I notice that my environment doesn't match the person that I am today. So it is time to move into a welcoming, healthy, prosperous, happy environment for me.

When you finish transforming your thought process, written now with only positive reasons, you will feel much more enthusiastic and energized to move forward and take the necessary steps to become or do. Every step of the way becomes more pleasurable because you have created a happy and positive future for yourself. What seemed to be big obstacles in the road are now the building stones and success is within reach! Congratulations! You truly do have the inner power to transform your life.

I have created a transformational workbook for my clients that enter the Honor Your Inner Treasures™ Program and as we go through the process they do simple, fun and motivating change processes. When they finish, only then the realization comes regarding how powerful it is to invest time into loving ourselves.

BELIEFS

All people have beliefs that help structure their lives. We know with great certainty that whatever we believe is true, and one of these beliefs is self-worth. People even determine their income based on their belief of self-worth. Your resume indicates exactly how much money you will make in the next year. When you review it and no changes have been made, you are hoping that inflation or the economy of the company you work for will determine the increase in the salary that you will be earning. Have you ever stopped to think about it? You are giving your power to another person to determine your growth, not only in your economy, but also your personal potential to do more, to become who you want to be.

I have worked with clients who are business owners feeling stressed out because of low funds, poor self-esteem and a lack of confidence. These issues not only impact their personal lives but also how their business grows. Those negative beliefs, ideas and limitations also have an impact on their earnings and the status of their finances, and all the people working for their company.

I remember working with Priti, a 43-year-old married woman. She emigrated to Canada from India, where she had received her degree as a software engineer. Once in Canada, Priti was able to obtain a position where she could use some of her education and experience. The reason I say 'some' of her education and experience is because when she came to see me for the first time she said that she was starting to feel bored with her job and not living up to her full potential. Priti felt that there were problems in the company that took too long to solve and required great work to make operations run more efficiently. Doing things the way the company had done for years was causing the same problems over and over again. She wanted to make a change and had a vision to do so.

However, Priti was quiet and didn't like to be the center of attention, so she kept to herself, trying to fit into the company's mold. Eventually, the conflict between shyness and wanting to change operations caused her a great deal of stress. She could not feel confident putting forth her suggestions. And although there was nothing I could do to help her with her software issues, I was able to help her build her confidence to act, speak, think and move forward. With those new positive traits, she was able to increase her self-esteem and recognize her own value.

Being foreign and fearing she might appear ignorant to others was one of Priti's greatest stumbling blocks. To offset this, I offered a metaphor. I asked her to consider the plastic casing that envelops the computer containing the software she created. Is that foreign? Obviously, the answer is no. The casing is just another part of the whole computer just as she, too, is part of the whole.

In creation nothing is foreign. We are all co-creating contributing our energy into the amazing universe we all live in. This is why it is so important that you truly live your lives from your inner treasures because underneath your fears and doubts you are pure potential, everyone has amazing positive energy to add to the whole.

We also worked on Priti's self-esteem and confidence by training her subconscious mind to act, feel and think the way the leader she desired to be would. The leader she wanted to be was one who confidently and clearly communicated her views, ideas and solutions with the tone of a manager. In just a few weeks Priti noticed she was expressing her ideas, asking questions and sharing her knowledge and experience without feeling timid. Most importantly, she noticed that her peers welcomed her ideas.

Eventually, Priti realized this company didn't have potential to grow and she was putting all of her potential in a box too small for her. She knew she was ready to move on with confidence.

That spark of inner realization of your personal self, and of how truly valuable your contribution is to everything you do, changes everything. You become confident to plan and live your life making decisions that feel right, and feel an inner peace because you gained control. Now, you have the power to do the things that are truly important to you. Once you learn to expand your consciousness beyond your fear, the limitation you had becomes limit-less.

In my upcoming book, *Limitless Beliefs - 7 Steps to Transcend into a Joyful and Abundant You*, you will find the how-to for this process. To purchase, learn more about the book, www.limitlessbeliefs.com or www.celinatioauthor.com.

YOUR LIFE IS YOUR DECISION AND YOUR CREATION

"Create your life experiences in such a way that the day you look back all you see is a magical garden of your own design that you can be proud of having imagined, lived, grown and created." – Celina Tio

"Really? Are you sure? Because I was told…" These are all comments based on a lack of confidence. This does not have to be you! You are able to declare your independence, power and freedom! To embrace the true and pure intention of creation!

I'll share with you the experience of Laura, a beautiful and intelligent woman who came to my office for help. As she introduced herself and explained the reason why she had made the appointment, I was amazed. At 32 years old, she was a successful fashion designer. Her passion, however, was singing and songwriting. What an amazing girl, and what a disparity in her professional career compared to her dreams.

Her narrative was sad due to many of her life's circumstances and events. Her self-esteem and confidence was at an all-time low after ending a relationship that was going nowhere. Now, she hoped to let go of all her little self. Laura wanted to have more confidence to make decisions and communicate her ideas and feelings, and she wanted to feel good about herself. Simply put, she wanted to live happily.

I could have told her how beautiful, amazing and intelligent I thought she was. I could have pointed out all the wonderful opportunities she could have in life or how much I admired her. But she wasn't there for me to tell her what most any friend would. She needed to know from her own heart, discovering and loving herself so that she could go through her life's journey knowing her essence.

At the end of her journey I asked Laura to write what she decided was most valuable about herself. She took a few days and sent me an e-mail describing her value as she perceived it. Imagine the courage it took to be so vulnerable. Without relying on anyone else's opinions, she confessed her own beauty, strength, warmth and intelligence. She had honored her inner treasures.

I have asked her permission to share this with you because I want you to know that it is also possible for you. She kindly and happily agreed because she felt she could help other people. Maybe that person today is you or someone you love.

"I value myself because I am a strong person who perseveres through hardship, and I have faith I will get through it. I value myself because I am loving and kind-hearted person. I value myself because I take care of those in need and treat them just as I would treat myself. I value myself because I am a hard worker and very motivated. I value myself because I am a good woman. I value myself because I have self-respect and integrity, and will not allow anyone to take that away. I value myself because I am humble in life. I value myself because I am a good sister, friend, daughter, and lover because I care for people's feelings. I value myself because of my relationship with God and how I want to continue to help myself be better. I value myself because I am a loving woman who shares love with everyone. I value myself because I can make people laugh and really bring out the best in them; this shows me how amazing I am. I value myself because even if I am scared or fearful I have courage to face those fears. I value myself because of my ability to forgive and make amends even when people have truly hurt me. I value my positive thinking and my ability to turn what can be a bad situation into a great one. I value myself because I am able to express my feelings and my emotions now in a calm and mature way. I value myself because any goal I set for myself I achieve, because I am willing to work hard. I value myself because I always keep on smiling even when the going gets tough. I value myself because I am beautiful, strong, smart, mature, funny, loving, and kind person."

- Laura, Toronto, Canada
Fashion Designer/ Singer and Songwriter, naturally from the heart.

APPRECIATION

If life were a coin, would you say it is less valuable when you are looking on the head side just because the imprinted value is on the other side and you can't see it?

The value of everything is found through deep appreciation. Lots of people walk through life with the expectation of being accepted and liked by others, but they suffer a great deal when the world around them doesn't show them what they expect. Start increasing your self-value by appreciating your life as it is in this moment. Even if your world looks or feels different than you'd like, there is value to be found. You can increase that value by describing it and saying thank you. At first, it might take some creativity if you have been depreciating things most of your life.

Let's think of something you do every day, like eating. All of us eat when we are hungry, but some also eat when anxious, nervous or depressed. There is even a name for this: comfort food. Comfort food is supposed to make you feel better when you eat it; however, nobody has ever said, "I was feeling sad and I ate a whole bowl of ice cream and now everything is fine! All of a sudden I feel loved and my finances have improved drastically with every spoonful of food I ate!" This would simply not be true.

On the other hand, when you eat because you feel hungry your body and mind feel better because they receive the nourishment needed. If you offer and share your meal and spend time in the company of family or friends, your soul is nourished as well. In preparing your meal, be grateful that you have the ingredients on hand needed to prepare the meal that will nourish every cell in your body. Imagine all the minerals, vitamins, proteins, carbohydrates and fibers that are present in what you are about to consume, and how you are benefiting from them. Thank the supermarket for having them available for you, and the people who've dedicated their life into growing them. Even thank the work you do that earns you the funds to buy your food. It's crucial to become aware of the dimension of what you are about to eat.

- Be grateful to the soil that has the perfect nutrients to grow your food.

- Be grateful to the sun and the water for adding their energy.

- Be grateful to the universe for having created a planet that contains everything you need.

- Be grateful for the beauty of the colors, textures and aromas of the vegetables, herbs or fruits, or a cup of coffee.

- Be grateful to the person who will share this meal with you.

- Be grateful that you can share your moment with that person and have each other's company.

- Be grateful that you have the ability to offer and share your meal.

- Be grateful that life is allowing this moment to sit, rest, replenish, keep each other's company and share whatever it is that needs to be shared at the moment.

By now, appreciation has started to flow from the heart and you will know if what you are about to eat is healthy for you. If you have to thank the chemicals named on the package that are so difficult to pronounce instead of the natural sweet aroma of a natural ripe tomato, you will know not to eat it. Your body will show you resistance. When appreciation flows from the heart, you will feel true comfort even when you drink plain water. Do it at your next meal. Do the same with your home, your family, your pet and your neighbor. Practicing heartfelt appreciation will change your perspective on life.

SELF-REALIZATION

"You have the power of pure energy within you to be, to do, to have, to accomplish, to become your dream." – Celina Tio

When you truly know your essence, everything changes easily. Your relationships are healthier by helping you grow with people who share your life's path. Life becomes pleasurable and enjoyable, and conflict and stress no longer emanate from you. You understand that ego makes peoples lives sad and full of problems, and that it drives competition, fear, war and destruction.

Knowing your essence also means the things that you're doing now are in line with what makes you feel happy. It's easy to identify if you're off balance because life no longer feels whole. You become aware of your energy and how it affects everything around you. You have a fresh understanding that you are part of creation, co-creating with all that makes us one.

You become more independent when you know your essence, investing into your wellbeing and happiness instead of things that have no value to your personal self. Rich and wealthy has a whole different meaning now. No more spending to do things or obtain things just because you feel bored or empty. You'll no longer feel the need to shop in an attempt to feel happy or, even worse, to look happy. You become independent and know that you are the only one responsible for how you are living your life, with no one else to blame. Vacationing to escape from reality is a thing of the past. Instead, you'll have the freedom to choose a destination that will give you enjoyment in everything from the planning to the adventure to the return.

At this point, inner peace has become real in your life and you'll have the self-realization that you truly are the creator of every moment in your life. Your future is right this moment, so make it amazing and wonderful. Move from the comfort spot of sameness, obedience and unhappiness. Walking on your self-pity will take you only to more of the same. It is time to tell yourself that you deserve to experience life, and to savor and indulge in the sweetness and pure love of creation. You deserve to feel free of unnecessary pain, have inner peace and feel truly loved.

Of course we all have sad moments in our lives. It is normal to experience loss and birth, laughter with tears of joy and also tears of sadness, and expansion and contraction. It is the Yin and Yang of life. What's important is what you do with it.

Your inner being has been waiting for you to listen truthfully to the pureness within. You are powerful beyond your comprehension, and have more than strength. You have the power of pure energy within you to be, to do, to have, to accomplish, and to become your dream. When I realized how powerful I was created to be, I stopped feeling small. I rid myself of unnecessary fears, choosing instead to be one with the moment. I learned to breathe moments out of love, peace and joy, and to share it with you and everyone around me. Let me help you heal. Allow me to guide you into that place of discovering and once and for all Honor Your Inner Treasures. Your life will be transformed.

www.honoryourinnertreasures.com

www.limitlessbeliefs.com

www.celinatioauthor.com

Have More Money, More Clients and More Freedom by Going Digital

Ashar Alam

As a savvy business owner, you understand that, whatever field you are in, whether it is chiropractic or real estate or Italian food, you are also in the business of marketing. You also know that the key to building and maintaining a successful business lies in keeping your marketing current and effective.

Many traditional forms of marketing simply don't measure up to the digital resources available today. If you haven't embraced this medium yet, you probably have seen competitors who do have a solid digital marketing strategy surging ahead of the pack (that includes you). If your market doesn't have a digital player yet, you have a golden opportunity to leave your competitors behind.

There are several steps you need to take to bring your business digitally up to par, and to get in position to set yourself apart. This chapter of The Authorities will focus on one very powerful digital marketing tool, search engine optimization (usually referred to as SEO). But, first, here's a broad look at exactly what digital marketing is.

DIGITAL MARKETING AUDIT

There are several different questions you should ask yourself in order to assess the current state of your business with respect to digital marketing. The most basic of these is: Do I have a website? If the answer is no, then you need to get one! This is as basic as it gets, but also as essential as it gets. A business's website is really the source from which all other digital marketing strategies flow.

If you do already have a business website, you can pat yourself on the back, but you are not out of the woods yet, not by a long shot. Begin to take a look at how well your site is serving your business:

- **Look critically at your site's URL/domain name.** A domain name like LocksmithSanDiego.com will have a leg up on competitors because it aligns well with what prospects for that business would be searching for on the web. It's also important to realize that a ".com" — or country-specific domains like ".ca" and ".co.uk" — is generally favored most by search engines and looked at as most legitimate by prospects.

- **Think about keywords that are relevant to your business from a customer's perspective.** Consider your own habits. What would you type into a search engine if you were looking for service in your field? The better optimized for these keywords your site is, the easier it will be for your prospects to find it.

- **Do some research to determine where your site ranks on popular search engines.** There is software that will do this, but it is simpler to do a Google search using likely keywords for your business. Does your site come up in the first page of results? The second? Again, think about how you use Google. How often do you navigate past the first or second page of search results? Most Googlers won't get too far past the first several results on the first page which, of course, is where you want your site to be. Optimized SEO can help make that happen.

- **How well does your site work when your prospects actually get there?** Can customers buy your product(s) directly from your website? If so, do they buy from you when they visit your website? How much time do they spend on your site once they get there? You can monitor these statistics, as well as other important website performance factors, with resources like Google Analytics; doing so is essential to getting the most out of your website.

- **Do you take advantage of other digital media channels**, such as social media (Facebook, Twitter, etc.), large retailers (Amazon, iTunes, etc.), mobile apps, and SMS marketing?

These questions and considerations represent a good starting point for assessing your business's digital marketing prowess, but they are really just scratching the surface. There are many more things to look into, whether it's calculating return on investment by estimating the lifetime value of your clients, setting up an infrastructure for capturing clients' email addresses and phone numbers, or optimizing your website for mobile devices.

It might seem like a lot to think about, and it is, but the more you apply these principles to your marketing strategy, the more your business will benefit. Everyone knows that putting in the effort is necessary to bringing about the desired result; what the above guidelines do is help you channel that effort strategically and productively.

SEO

Speaking of using your effort wisely, one of the most important aspects of digital marketing is SEO. You will definitely want to funnel some of your digital marketing efforts into SEO to ensure that your prospects have the opportunity to find out about your business.

The name "search engine optimization" is fairly self-explanatory — it refers to optimizing a website so that it's easy for a search engine to find it. However, properly executing this concept is not as simple as the concept itself is. Keywords, like the ones discussed above, must be well-integrated into the very coding of the various pages on your site. There are also several other factors, such as back links, social markers and likability — discussed in further detail below — that contribute to how your site will fare on the search engines.

Crucially, all of this must be done in a strategic way. Obviously catering to keywords can lead to negative repercussions. Search engines will take action against those who blatantly game the system, banishing them to obscure sections of search results and dealing a severe blow to their digital marketing schemes.

"FREE" ADVERTISING

In the sense that it requires time and effort, and potentially the paid help of a specialist, SEO is not free. However, compared to the level of paid advertising you would have to employ to get the same level of visibility, SEO is a terrific bargain. And, it generates a very strong return on investment (ROI).

In terms of search engines, organic SEO can actually be much more valuable than paid advertising, even without considering cost. The major search engines — Google, Yahoo! and Bing — display unpaid listings on the same results page as paid ones. Plus, local business results are typically included with national ones. Most of the time, web users simply ignore the paid listings, which display on a different part of the page —either off to the side or above the organic listings. (Again, think about your own behavior in such situations — you may have never even noticed that Google displays paid listings alongside the unpaid ones you naturally look for.)

People rely on search engines to provide something like an unbiased survey of what's out there, and paid ads don't fit very well into this expectation. On the other hand, a "real" listing that pops up prominently in the results is more appealing. Websites that pop up toward the beginning of the results do so because they are well optimized for search engines. This is the key to SEO. The effort required is invisible to the customer, and a prominent search engine result comes with built-in legitimacy.

WHAT ARE SEARCH RESULTS BASED ON?

You've already seen how SEO starts with keywords. Your search engine ranking will partly be dependent upon where these keywords show up on your site and how much competition there is for the keywords you target. As a general guideline, strategically placed keywords should not exceed 1-2% of the copy on your site.

"Longtail" keywords, such as "best DUI attorney in Buffalo New York," can help sites succeed in a competitive market, although incorporating them will probably require outside help; for example, from a specialty marketing firm. Because SEO is so important these days, many firms specialize in assisting companies in this way. This is, of course, an extra expense — as discussed above, good SEO is not free — but for many markets its benefits will hugely outweigh the costs.

A more stripped down way to achieve something similar is to incorporate a blog into your website. Blogs continually generate fresh, keyword-rich content, and can help drive traffic to your website. For many businesses, generating blog posts is a more doable in-house operation for enhancing SEO, although it is also something that can be outsourced, and typically for a much lower price than that of hiring a marketing firm.

There are other specific attributes besides keywords that are important as well. Some of these are still intimately related to keywords, while others are completely separate. Google will determine rankings according to:

Authority – How authoritative is a given site in relation to the search term? Has it been highly ranked in the results of this search term for a long time?

Relevance – How popular is this search? Is it generating a lot of web traffic? Are many people searching for these specific keywords?

Competition – What sites mention these keywords? What sites prominently feature these keywords (i.e., in the title or domain name)? What are the SEO-related qualities, both on-page and off-page, of these sites? For example, age, rank, back links (see next bullet point), and prominence and density of keywords.

Back links – These are like citations in an article, and function somewhat as votes for a site. How many other sites are linking back to a given page? Are the sites that are linking to the page in question themselves high-SEO sites? Poor quality back links can be worse than no links at all, as this is exactly the type of thing Google cracks down on. Spammy back links can cause a site to be thrown into the Google "sandbox," meaning it is dropped from the top hundred search results.

Social markers – Does this site have connections with social media sites like Facebook, Twitter and LinkedIn? Are users linking back to it on these platforms?

Likability – Many different measures determine the likability of a site, such as:

- Time spent on page – How long do visitors to a given page stay there before navigating away? Videos are a great way to increase visitors' time spent on your site. A live chat feature is another way to keep visitors from navigating away from a page.

- Bounce rate – The percentage of visitors who leave the site rather than navigate to other pages within the site. A high bounce rate means people who visit your site are not finding a reason to stay there.

- Scroll rate – Do visitors scroll down through a page, or leave directly after it loads without scrolling through? Make sure each page has enough content to engage a visitor. Most pages should have a minimum of 500 words. Meeting that word limit is one easy way to address this issue.

- Grammar – Poor grammar can be a marker of regurgitated content. Sites with high likability will not have grammatical errors.

- Downloads – A great way to increase likability of a page. Offering PDF documents, MP3s, and/or video files as downloads helps to engage visitors to your site.

SEO is certainly a multi-layered topic, and the larger world of digital marketing is even more intensive. This chapter has given you several simple action steps you should take immediately to better market your business online. To learn more about how digital marketing can build your business significantly, you may want to visit thebookondigitalmarketing.com.

In the meantime, look back through the audit above, and through the bulleted list of SEO principles. Satisfactorily dealing with these various aspects of digital marketing is often an ongoing project for successful businesses. There are many angles from which to approach it, which means finding a place to dive in is easy — there are so many options.

SEO in particular is a long term consideration. Working your way into a favorable spot in search engine rankings can take time. But, as discussed above, truly earning a prominent organic listing is highly valuable exposure for a business, so it's a worthy goal to pursue.

And, now that you have some valuable information about how to go about it, go out and spread the word about your business!

Create the Life of Your Dreams

The Savvy Investor's Ultimate Guide to Wholesaling Real Estate

Dexter Montgomery & Pamela Montgomery

Many people look to real estate investment as an enjoyable, flexible, and dependable way to generate income. Whether that means supplementing a day job or completely transforming the way you spend your time and fund your lifestyle, you might be one of these people. Even in a changing housing market, real estate continues to represent an essential part of the economy – neighborhoods transition, young people grow up, properties continue to be bought and sold; great deals are always out there.

The allures of investing in real estate are many – being your own boss, making your own hours, earning more than you ever have before, setting your own financial goals and having the means to meet them – but, while it can be extremely rewarding, entering into real estate can also be very challenging.

The inexperienced will not know the many ins and outs of buying, selling, renting, and rehabbing properties: everything from the appropriate lingo (a must if you want to be taken seriously) to housing market trends and the function of different specialists with whom you must work to be successful. That doesn't even include general entrepreneurial skills like setting goals and educating yourself; these things are absolutely essential to success in real estate investment as well.

As in many other fields, experience can be invaluable in investment, but knowing the lay of the land before you ever get your feet wet is essential. The process of trial and error is not so desirable when an "error" means losing a substantial portion of a large amount of money you have invested.

If you are serious about establishing a career or side-career in real estate investment, you will most certainly make mistakes and experience hardships along the way and, if you are patient and resilient, you will learn from them. However, you have to put the time and effort in before you get involved to ensure that you know what you're doing.

Real estate coaches and seminar speakers will often talk about all the mistakes they made when they were starting out. In this field, that means losing money, sometimes a lot of it. Consider yourself lucky to have the option of using their advice and expertise to help you avoid these same mistakes. Some of this information is free, but immersing yourself in the necessary knowledge will require an investment. You must trust that, if you find the right programs, seminars, coaches, books, and other resources, it is worth every penny.

You will not get to where you need to be by reading one chapter on the subject, but it's a great start. If you're serious about pursuing this opportunity that you know can make your life better and help you realize your goals, you will use a resource like this chapter as a diving board into the "deep end," so to speak, where you can really educate and immerse yourself.

FORMS OF REAL ESTATE INVESTMENT

On a basic level, a big part of diving into real estate investment is a decision about what form of investment to pursue. Eventually, as you grow with your business, you might very well want to expand your efforts, trying different types of investments and determining which ones make the most sense for you and for different types of situations. However, when you are just starting, it is important not to overextend yourself. You will do well to focus on only one type of investment.

What really differentiates one kind of real estate investment from another is the "exit strategy" for a given property. If you think of your initial acquisition of the property as your "entrance," and your plans for that property as your "exit," you begin to see that there are many different options. Planning your exit strategy before you acquire a property is essential to understanding how you will profit from the transaction.

These are the most common ways to profit from a real estate investment:

- **Wholesale**: Acquiring a property at a favorable price from a motivated seller and quickly reselling it to a motivated buyer. You might be selling the property to someone who will then pursue one of the following strategies.

- **Rental**: Acquiring a property and holding on to it for the long term, earning profit on it by leasing to a tenant.

- **Rehab**: Also known as "flipping" a property. It's more of a long term project than wholesale buying and selling. Rehabbing involves acquiring a distressed property and fixing it up to bring up its value, then reselling it.

These various forms of investment differ in several ways, from timeline to resources required to marketplace appropriateness, and many more. A certain property may be better suited to one of these investment methods than to the others. Comparing your expected costs to your expected income will help you decide which is most appropriate.

For example, rehabbing a property balances the combined cost of acquiring it and bringing it back to life against what someone will pay you for it once you've done so. Renting is only prudent when you know the income from your tenant will cover your costs – that includes acquiring, holding, and maintaining the property.

If you intend to wholesale a property, you must have a good understanding of how quickly you can expect to sell it, and at what price. Simply holding on to a property will be one of your costs, due to property tax, so how quickly you sell will determine how much you can profit from that sale. Likewise, buying and reselling a property will, of course, only be profitable to you if your sell price is higher than your buy price. Researching comparable sales, both from a timing and a pricing perspective, will help give you a read on this. The better you know the neighborhood you're buying and selling in, the better you can understand what to expect.

Other factors to consider, both when deciding between types of investment and when determining whether or not to buy in at all, include:

- **Financial risk**: How much are you willing to take on?

- **ROI** (Return on Investment): How much money do you expect to make from this deal, and how quickly do you expect to make it?

- **Your time**: How much time will you have to research the deal? How much time will you have to devote to managing/fixing up/appraising/marketing the property?

- **Your effort**: How much effort are you willing to put into the above considerations?

- **Financing**: Where will the money you are investing come from?

WHOLESALING

As discussed above, dipping your toes into the water of real estate development is a great place to start but, if you're serious about pursuing it, you will eventually dive in all the way. The rest of this chapter will discuss in greater detail one specific facet of real estate investment: wholesaling. You'll want to continue to seek out additional resources to get deeper into the others.

Wholesaling is a great entry point because getting into it doesn't require as much money up front as some of the other types of investment do. As mentioned above, a wholesaler is essentially a "middle man" between a motivated buyer and a motivated seller. Let's dig a little deeper into who these people are and how they are relevant to you, the investor.

Motivated Buyers

To those without a lot of real estate experience, the idea of a property buyer might bring to mind a family buying a home, or a business owner buying a commercial space to use as a storefront or office. Images in media or perhaps from personal experience probably bring to mind buyers concerned about location, and looking for a space they will "fall in love with." You might picture a couple that wants space to raise children and access to good schools, or a store owner looking for an area with good visibility and ample room for storage.

Although these kinds of things are important to certain types of real estate deals, they are not so relevant to the wholesaler. The family and the business owner would not be examples of motivated buyers. Rather, a motivated buyer is someone with ready access to cash, looking for a good investment him- or herself. A motivated buyer will "fall in love" with a property if the numbers indicate that it represents a good business deal.

Finding and attracting these motivated buyers becomes much easier when you are offering them an attractive price. This is why understanding the market is so important in a wholesale deal. You have to be sure that, when you buy a property, you will be able to resell it at a price that is low enough to easily and quickly attract motivated buyers and high enough to provide you with a profit.

Offering great deals to motivated buyers – and handling transactions professionally and ethically – will encourage those buyers to come back to you again and again, looking for more opportunities to buy from you. As your business grows, you can begin to put together a database of names and build a network.

In fact, networks of this kind already exist in many forms, and getting access to them is a great first step to finding motivated buyers. Joining a local real estate investment club is one way to meet other investors and begin to build your network. You can also meet investors by attending property auctions. Networking in this way is an invaluable part of getting started in property wholesaling.

Motivated Sellers

Let's talk about the other side of the equation, the motivated seller. Just as a motivated buyer is someone with cash in hand, looking to buy quickly, rather than someone carefully searching for a property to "fall in love with," a motivated seller is not somebody who would like to sell a property, or is maybe considering it, but somebody who has to sell, for one reason or another.

A motivated seller will have a strong reason (usually a financial one) compelling him or her to sell. Falling behind on a mortgage, suffering a personal hardship like divorce or loss of a job, and inheriting an unwanted property are examples. As a wholesaler, you are in a position to solve a problem for a motivated seller. You can take a property off the seller's hands and move it to someone who wants it.

In this way, real estate wholesaling is really a win-win-win situation. The seller gets rid of an unwanted or unsustainable property, the buyer finds a good investment and you, the wholesaler, essentially earn a fee for bringing these two parties together. You might think of this as a sort of "finder's fee."

So how do you find these motivated sellers? There are several different strategies you might consider. These sellers have to know that you are available to provide them with this service, so marketing yourself is essential.

Advertising is an important way to get onto a potential seller's radar, be it through the newspaper, the internet, or even a sign along the road.

You can also proactively look for properties by combing through listings or by driving or walking around in an area and hunting for "For Sale" signs. When physically going around and looking at properties, seek out distressed or vacant homes and "FSBO" (For Sale by Owner) signs. While searching through listings, keep an eye out for expiring listings and those labeled things like "Handyman Special" or "Needs Work".

Here again, networking can come in handy, as working with real estate agents who search the MLS (Multiple Listing Service) can give you access to these types of listings. Another group, sometimes known as "bird dogs," can be a great resource too. Bird dogs are people who pass on good deals to wholesalers, for a fee. As with motivated buyers, if you are respectful and ethical in your dealings with real estate agents and bird dogs, they will want to continue to work with you and bring deals to you.

If you find a property you're interested in, you can send a postcard or a letter to the owners, offering to help solve their problem. If need be, you can find names and addresses in government property tax records.

You may make many, many offers before one is accepted, so patience is incredibly important to finding success in wholesaling. Once you get some momentum behind your business and build your network, you will have more resources for finding good opportunities for investment, but when you dive in you will need the determination to overcome rejection.

KEEP LEARNING!

Now that you know a little bit about investing in real estate, and specifically the strategy of wholesaling, you are in a great position to build on that knowledge. If the financial flexibility and excitement of buying and selling property grabs your interest, you will want to dig much deeper. There are so many resources to seek out, from books to internet forums to seminars to coaches and mentors. Don't cut corners; continue to educate yourself and you'll be in great shape to dive into this exciting field.

Enter Into a Passionate Relationship with Your Own Life

SILVANA AVRAM

Have you ever wondered whether there is more to life than meets the eye? Do you feel that despite all your achievements true fulfilment still eludes you?

Join me on this transformational journey where you will learn to see yourself and your life in a different light.

- You will find out how to ask the right questions.
- You will learn to identify the main reason why you find yourself trapped in the same vicious circle.
- You will redefine the true meaning of being and uncover the source of deep fulfilment.
- You will be able to decide whether you are ready to embark on the journey to personal fulfilment.

My passionate plea to you is to allow this introduction to the secret of lasting fulfilment to work as a powerful catalyst for you. Should you want to explore the topics addressed here in more depth I invite you to read my book "Being You And Loving You – The Ultimate Guide To Fulfilment" – where I guide you through twelve life changing steps to true fulfilment. Together with the book you will also find plenty of free materials, insights and support at www.BeingYouAndLovingYou.com

It is the aim of this chapter to empower you to start your journey to true fulfilment. Are you ready? Let's dive in!

YOUR JOURNEY TO FULFILMENT STARTS WITH ASKING THE RIGHT QUESTIONS

"The Universe contains three things that cannot be destroyed; Being, Awareness and LOVE"

— Deepak Chopra

"What is the meaning of life?" Human beings have searched for an answer to this question for millennia. Sages, philosophers, religious figures and scientists have all put forward their hypotheses, and each interpretation added yet another nuance to a mystery that remains as fascinating and as alluring as it has always been.

So: "Why are we here?" And why is it that this most important question of all is also one of the most avoided? Perhaps we have long accepted that there is no answer to it. Perhaps facing this question feels so…unsettling that we prefer to bury it under more…urgent matters. Like finding a job and paying the next bill.

I put to you another possibility. I believe that "Why are we here?" is indeed an unanswerable question. At least for the time being. And so is *"What is the meaning of life?"*

Why? Because they are too vast...and too vague!

Does that mean I am advising you to drop the questioning altogether and simply get on with your life? No, not at all! Not if you want to live a joyous, meaningful life. Not if you are looking for true fulfilment. In fact, if this is what you are after, it is vitally important to keep questioning.

But you must learn to ask the right questions.

I believe that each one of us must start with the more manageable "Why *am I* here?" or "What is the meaning of *my* life?"

I believe that each one of us must take responsibility for our own answers.

You see, when you allow someone else to answer these questions for you, you give away your power (and with that your responsibility). You may like a particular answer/ philosophy for a while and you may find it resonates with you – you may even dedicate your life to promoting it – but it will still not be yours – and as such it will not fully transform your life, it will not bring you the fulfilment you crave. You may read as many books as you want and you may attend endless wonderful seminars...They will all help you feel good for a while and you are sure to get some valuable insight. But no person and no book can truly change your life for you. Only when you find the strength and the courage to stay with the question of meaning long enough to allow for your own answer to be born in you, will you find the infinite joy and freedom that come from knowing. It is only *your own* answer that will truly transform *your life*. It is owning that answer that brings true fulfilment.

If your life is a riddle, the only way to fully - fill it… is to find your own answer to it.

Now that you know where to start…how do you actually do it?

You can find your own answer by asking the right questions, either on your own or by engaging in a philosophical dialogue with friends and other people interested in the same quest for meaning. You must be patient and tenacious, and not give up at the first signs of exhaustion or disappointment. After all, the question of meaning is the most challenging question of all, and many choose to avoid it altogether. But if you stay with it, if you make it an intrinsic part of your journey, sooner or later you will be rewarded.

You will not be alone in your endeavour. One of the most famous of the Delphic maxims inscribed in the pronaos (forecourt) of the Temple of Apollo at Delphi, Ancient Greece, and quoted by many, most famously by Socrates as the main character in Plato's dialogues, was *"Know Thyself"*. Through the ages there have been many who have embarked on this arduous journey.

Today, there is a modern variant of the life-transforming dialogues left to posterity by Plato: the coaching dialogue. The Philosopher is replaced by the more modest Coach. They are similar, however, in that the Coach, like the Greek philosopher but unlike a religious figure or a mentor, is not providing the answers. Instead, she or he is merely providing you with the right questions, gently challenging you when you go off track and often holding a symbolic mirror in which you start to see your true reflection and find your own answers.

It is a true measure of our 21st Century's *Age of Knowledge* that Coaching has become such an accessible experience. Perhaps this is a sign that more and more amongst us are ready and willing to stay with the question of meaning and find the true purpose of our lives. Perhaps more and more people are ready to embark on the journey to true fulfilment. Are you?

BEING SUCCESSFUL IS NOT THE SAME AS SUCCEEDING AT BEING

> *"What makes you think human beings are sentient and aware? There's no evidence for it. Human beings never think for themselves, they find it too uncomfortable. For the most part, members of our species simply repeat what they are told – and become upset if they are exposed to any different view. The characteristic human trait is not awareness but conformity.."*
>
> — *Michael Crichton*

> *"I am a human being, not a human doing. Don't equate your self-worth with how well you do things in life. You aren't what you do. If you are what you do, then when you don't...you aren't."*
>
> — *Dr. Wayne Dyer*

Before we proceed to consider what your journey to true fulfilment might look like when you embark on a path of enquiry and examination, I would like you to briefly stop and take a look at your life right now.

Do you love your life? Do you love yourself? Do you feel deep gratitude and awe about who you are? Do you feel blissful, fulfilled and radiant, sharing your wisdom and your light with everyone else, in compassion?

Chances are that you don't.

Chances are that you don't even believe this is possible!!

But if it were possible, would you like to feel like this? Would you like to live your life with absolute joy, and share your happiness with others?

I hope your answer to that last question is yes.

If it is, you have already taken the first step to fulfilment.

You see, most people have already given up on personal fulfilment. Most people have somehow fallen into the trap of believing that there is nothing more to life than work, duty, supporting family and friends, and the occasional recreation. It may sound incredible, but most people have convinced themselves that life is more about sacrifice and suffering than about being happy. If asked, of course everyone would say they want to be happy. Yet most people spend their lives doing things that take them farther and farther away from being joyful and fulfilled.

Most people spend most of their lives *doing* things. In fact doing so many things that they don't have the time to stop and ask *why* they are doing them.

Most people spend their lives doing so many things that they forget to Be.

But how can I forget to be? I hear you ask.

What else is there to 'being' that I haven't got already? Is it not enough that I am…alive? How can I be …being? How can I Be more?

You see…rocks and trees and animals are too. They exist. Life flows through them and expresses through them without encountering much opposition. They are pure expressions of life.

And so are we. Except for the fact that we also have the wonderful gifts of thought, of mind…of consciousness.

I want you to consider that maybe, just maybe, for us humans it is not enough to be alive, to truly Be. If it were, we would all be happy – or at least at ease. We would not ask questions. We would not search for more.

What makes us different is that we have the gift of being able to be aware of being. It is this gift, and whether or not we choose to use it, that makes all the difference.

In order to truly Be as a human being you must be aware of who you are – of your potential. You must get involved in "being", become responsible for your "being", become the co-creator of your life.

When, on the other hand, we choose not to use the gift of awareness, we spend most of our lives doing things, being alive without truly being aware of the mystery, the complexity and the beauty of our being. We allow doing to take over, we throw ourselves into doing with a vengeance, seeking solace in temporary achievements that often leave us emptier than before.

Why and how does this happen? When we live without fully being present to our own lives, to our own being, we function on automatic pilot much of the time. Most of the functions we perform require so little of our conscious input that we get used to being disengaged. It's easier. We do the minimum and we get by. If we are "lucky" we can spend our whole life without having to account for the huge lack of …presence in it. For the most part, everyone is doing the same, and we are covered. No one will know. No one will dare ask.

But is that truly "lucky"? Is our life really about "getting by"?

If it were, mere survival would qualify as fulfilment. You would already and at all times feel fulfilled. Yet most of us know deep down inside our hearts that our lives must be more than just survival.

Perhaps our life is about success?

The difference between success and fulfilment is that success, as it tends to be defined, is still at the level of doing. You can become successful by following instructions and still staying on autopilot. In fact, the more autopilot-friendly the system you follow, the more successful you probably are in that particular area.

It is a common mistake to equate success with fulfilment. Many people who do, realize that success has not brought them the fulfilment they wished for. Many of these people spend years wondering where they went wrong and what's missing.

Our society seems to conspire to push us towards a narrowly defined form of success that rarely allows any space for true fulfilment. In other words, our misinterpretations are not entirely our fault. We are taught from early on to play by the (widely accepted) rules. We trust our parents and our teachers, and we unwittingly follow in their footsteps. We keep ourselves busy doing so many things that we have little time for self-exploration or personal inquiry, for Being. It is this restless drive for doing more and more that slowly but surely derails us from the only achievement that matters: understanding, accepting and expressing – in fact Being - our true self. Unless we stop to ask the right questions we don't even realise what we are missing.

To sum it up, success in doing cannot lead to fulfilment, for the simple reason that it involves operating at a different level.

To achieve true fulfilment you must operate at the level of Being.

It is not being successful at doing that will make you feel fulfilled.

To be fulfilled you must succeed at Being.

* * * *

So far we have learnt that in order to be fulfilled you must start by asking the right questions: "What is the meaning of my life?" "Why am I here?"

Tackling these and similar questions of meaning helps you become aware: aware that there is more to life than meets the eye; aware that as a human being it is not enough to be alive…Nor is it enough to be doing many things.

We then looked at what happens when you don't ask these questions. When you avoid questioning the true meaning of your life you get sucked into a life of endless doing with very little time for Being – and hence, with very little or no chance of feeling fulfilled.

For most people the question of meaning is an intimidating one, and one they'd rather put aside. After all, why take responsibility for one's life when it seems easier to just get by? Many people "succeed" in avoiding this question altogether. They also miss the opportunity of living deeply fulfilling, joyful lives. For others, something happens that forces them to wake up to it. It could be an unexpected turn of fate, a tragic event, even a major bonus, like winning the lottery, that pushes them to take a deeper look in the mirror. At those times they discover that there is a whole new dimension to 'being' that they were completely ignoring before. It is then up to them to embark on a journey of discovery that should ultimately lead them to true fulfilment.

There is, of course, a more natural, organic way that comes when you simply decide to take responsibility for your life and actively explore the gifts it promises to offer. You do it because you realize this is the only way you are going to feel truly happy and fulfilled. You do it because you want to be a co–creator in your life and express your full potential.

Along the way you may need the help of a friend, a sage or a coach – and you may be able to help others – but ultimately each one of us must find our own answers in order to express the true richness of our lives.

Once you are on the path to fulfilment there is no going back. You taste the ecstasy of being alive. Everything thereafter is a miraculous discovery, a wonderful adventure, a self-affirming deed and a deeply fulfilling expression of who you are. You have been kissed by life.

TRUE FULFILMENT COMES FROM AN AUTHENTIC AND LOVING RELATIONSHIP WITH YOUR LIFE

"The first step toward change is awareness. The second step is acceptance."

— Nathaniel Branden

We have established that in order to find true fulfilment you must be able to start with the right question and you must be able and willing to stay with it until you find your own answer. This is no easy journey. But it is the only one that will get you to true fulfilment. And as such, it is the most exciting journey of all.

If you are looking for deeper fulfilment, if you have started to realise that fulfilment will not come from doing more "stuff", chances are that you are already awakening to the possibility of an infinitely richer you. It does not matter how long it took you to get to this point. What matters is that you are ready: ready to embark on the beautiful, empowering, liberating and ultimately fulfilling journey of Being; ready to Be. Now.

Congratulations! Let the journey begin!

* * * *

As a coach, I can never get tired of seeing my clients find true joy and meaning in their lives. It often feels as if I watch them learn how to fly. And when they take off on their own…The sense of unlimited potential, freedom and happiness that comes with finding your own answer to the mystery of life is truly indescribable. One must experience it to be able to understand it.

But, if you will allow me, I would like to share with you what you might expect along the way.

There are two essential ingredients that will ensure a successful journey.

1. In order to be fulfilled you must first learn to Be.
2. Then you must learn how to Love Being.

As we touched upon earlier, truly Being requires presence and awareness.

True fulfilment comes when you and your life become one. When you live passionately…fully. To be one with life you must first wake up to Being; you must be aware of who you really are.

To start with, this will involve exploring your strengths, your talents, your gifts. It will mean looking at what makes you *you*, what makes you unique. In case you are already backing off in fear, rest assured. Every one of us is unique. Your special features, your memories and stories, your thoughts and feelings, your desires and dreams…all these make you a world unto itself, a uniquely beautiful expression of life, an exquisite original work of art in constant motion. There is no one else in the entire universe like you. There has never been and there will never be! You just have to muster the courage to embrace this truth! And allow it to transform you! It will help to have someone else hold the mirror, but once you learn to look at yourself in this way you will be able to see your life in a different light.

(To learn more about how you can embrace and celebrate your uniqueness visit www.BeingYouAndLovingYou.com)

It will then be important to find ways to truly express who you are; to listen to your heart and let it teach you everything you had tried to forget. Becoming aware of your thought patterns and connecting with your deepest emotions will enable you to re-define yourself. Then you can move one step further and try your hand at re-creating who you are. Being you is the gift you were given. Accepting this gift and then bettering it will be the gift you give back to life. How wonderful. This is pure creation. It's a miraculous process. Let it be fun!

At this point you should be ready to start thinking of how you could share your gift with others. This will become your purpose. That's when the real magic begins. And with it, true joy.

This is the point on your journey when your love relationship with life truly begins. The intimate loving relationship that you have managed to build with yourself expands into a passionate love affair with your life.

Now that you have become the co-creator of your life you must allow yourself to fall in love with your creation. You and your life must become one. This means moving from living your life into allowing your life to live, to express through you. You must be in awe of your life, you must respect it and cherish it and place it above anything else. Because your life is your gift to yourself and to the world. Because your life is the most intimate expression of who you are.

Loving your life is acknowledging and loving the infinite potential that you are. Loving your life with passion will teach you how to love every life with passion – will help you connect with every other life in compassion and joy. Knowing that you have expressed the best of you gives you the licence to feel free, to feel happy, to feel fulfilled.

When you live your life with this intensity there is a point where you will have to lose yourself to find yourself. That is when you must confront your deepest fear. Just as you have learnt to love yourself you must prepare to lose yourself. This is your ultimate act of sacrifice. You understand that your life does not belong to you. And this makes you love it even more. Now living your best possible life truly becomes your mission – and the only measurement of feeling true fulfilment.

You are now close, very close in fact, to fulfilment. You have already had glimpses of it – and you have started to feel its presence more and more poignantly. It is a mysterious, evasive feeling but one that is constant, and constantly making you blush. It permeates your life like a subtle perfume, like the light filling a room – like the presence of joy.

Your wonderful ability to be has now become a living example for others to see. By being you and fulfilling your mission you gift the world with your presence, and your life is the very proof of your fulfilment.

You inspire, you touch other lives and you share your wisdom and your joyful awareness with ease.

You live your life with the profound and blissful awareness of having achieved true fulfilment and the immense gratitude of having been able to do so.

* * * *

How does that feel? I hope you were able to get a glimpse of what it might mean to walk the journey to fulfilment. Often the transformation that takes place is difficult to put into words.

Suffice it to say that in this magical process you and your life will be completely transformed.

You enter a true partnership with life. You fall in love with your life and you become a co-creator of your life. That is the true meaning of being one with life. You live passionately – vibrantly. You express through your life and your life expresses through you.

To love being, to be in love with your life, is to step beyond being you into the miraculous field of living your life in service to Life – of giving your life as a gift back to Life. Everything you do at this level enriches you and enhances your life while affirming Life itself.

True fulfilment comes from being authentic and accomplishing your potential – thus fulfilling and honouring the unique opportunity that your life is.

(Explore more and get inspired with the wealth of insights and materials on the topic of being you, loving you and transcending you…that you will find at: www.BeingYouAndLovingYou.com)

LIVING A FULFILLING LIFE: IF NOT NOW, WHEN?

"Waking up is not a selfish pursuit of happiness, it is a revolutionary stance, from the inside out, for the benefit of all beings in existence."

– Noah Levine

We have explored together what it takes to embark on the journey to personal fulfilment.

We saw that it all starts with asking the right questions. We looked at what might happen when we fail to ask these questions. Then we had a glimpse at what to expect once we embark on this journey. I suppose the only question left is…Are you in?

You see… You either are or you aren't feeling fulfilled right now. And if you aren't, you are faced with a serious choice. True personal fulfilment involves presence and passion. You can't tell your life "I will live you tomorrow" or "I will love you tomorrow." You can't tell your mission, your purpose "I will be with you later." You have to be ready, open to it now. You have to commit to living your best possible life now.

The journey to fulfilment is not the easiest. It does require courage, honesty, a deep sense of wonder, the desire to overcome fears and the capacity to accept life's ephemeral and mysterious nature – and love it all the more for it.

To truly know fulfilment you must make the transition from living at the doing level to living at the Being level. Being successful has nothing to do with being fulfilled. Succeeding at Being has everything to do with it.

To truly succeed at Being you must go on a journey of self-discovery, and learn to celebrate your uniqueness, your richness, your unique expression, your feelings. You must learn to become a conscious co-creator of your life and then find the best ways to share your creation.

With this you move towards learning to love yourself and falling in love with your life. Once you learn to love yourself you must overcome your fear of losing yourself. This gives you the freedom to share yourself with the world.

By doing this you become an inspiration to others. You share the light of awareness with others. Finally you give back your life to Life with and for others – and in this you find ultimate fulfilment.

I don't know of a more wondrous journey – or one that is more worth it. You have been invited. The door has been opened for you. But only you can walk this journey and make your life the most extraordinary adventure of all. It is your life. Will you make it your fulfilment?

FINAL THOUGHT

If these pages have inspired you, you are probably ready to embark on the journey to fulfilment. Sometimes all we need is for someone to point the way. At other times we need someone to hold our hand as we learn how to fly on our own. I believe that Coaching can do that.

I believe that we live in a world where holding hands and learning from each other is soon becoming the norm. It is the only way in which we will be able to move forward. It is the only way in which we will learn, together, to truly Be. To be in love with our lives and to honour our potential. To find deep and lasting fulfilment. To share our richness and our beauty with everyone else, in joy. You can do it! See you there!

* * * *

Silvana is a successful Inspirational Coach, philosopher, writer and teacher.

More than anything else Silvana is a passionate human being driven by a deep commitment to create a better, happier world for everyone. She founded Life Coaching with Silvana to reach out and make her own contribution through empowering individuals to embrace and fulfil their potential, follow their dreams and live life with joy and gratitude. Silvana currently lives in the UK and divides her time between writing, coaching, group coaching, teaching, travelling, supporting humanitarian projects and conducting workshops and seminars.

To get in touch with Silvana, to know more about her Coaching practice, her projects and the events she organizes visit www.LifeCoachingWithSilvana.com

To get her book "Being You and Loving You – The Ultimate Guide To Fulfilment" together with free materials and more insights into the topic of fulfilment visit: www.BeingYouAndLovingYou.com

Evolution of Consciousness for the Entrepreneur

Accelerate Your Consciousness, Master Your Life

Audree Tara Weitzman

"Be the change that you wish to see in the world."

– Mahatma Gandhi

"With great power comes great responsibility"

– Voltaire, Uncle Ben, Spiderman

We have been through the Industrial Evolution, the Scientific Evolution and the Technological Evolution. Now is the time for the Evolution of Consciousness. A term prevalent in the personal growth and transformational communities, the Evolution of Consciousness comes out of the ever growing New Age movement. It involves the process of self-awareness and the awakening of the human mind. In truth, it is about personally understanding and awakening to our own behaviors, belief systems and the answers to two critical questions: "Does this serve me?" and "Do I want to live this way?

What does this have to do with you, the entrepreneur? Self-awareness can be a powerful tool in the development of your success.

YOUR THOUGHTS AND BEHAVIORS CREATE YOUR REALITY

We are facing a critical time in our human history. I say critical because our economy, ecology and the human race are struggling for survival. The stress of maintaining your life and excelling to a better way of living has become unbalanced in the "me" culture that we have become. This struggle for survival has an effect on a personal scale: financial hardships, loss of jobs, market crashes, housing devaluations and a lack of well being. We are living fearful lives and have lost connections to both our inner selves and the outer world around us.

You can say that this cataclysmic way of thinking has gone on for centuries. Why do we now need to become aware of our behaviors and how we live? It is because all that we have accomplished, created and discovered can now be utilized for the self-preservation of the planet and the human race. We can take what we have learned and create a way of life that supports community, growth, prosperity and the regeneration of a damaged ecology. I see the Evolution of Consciousness as a coming together of all the past evolutionary processes, and the using of our higher awareness to shift and change the way we live in the world. We can then create a world where we are living to our fullest potential.

So, how does an entrepreneur fit into this world of instability and chaos? Every entrepreneur is a visionary. You think outside the box. Your thoughts and belief systems control who you are and what you become. You are looking for a way to succeed beyond what is expected of you. At the same time, however, everyone else in your life has his or her limited thoughts and belief systems. The outside support for your great adventure (owning your own business) is, therefore, weak, or sometimes non-existent. The evolution of your consciousness and the awareness of your mind's thoughts and belief systems will be your strongest supporter on the road to success.

Human beings are automatically hardwired for failure. It is ingrained in our being that we are less than perfect. Most people live their lives with minds full of negative thoughts. Those thoughts keep telling them they are not good enough, or that they do not have the power to create an amazing life. In fact, those thoughts often say "you do not deserve to have an amazing life". On average, people walk through life sick, poor and lacking enthusiasm or joy for life. They go to school, and then work at a job that meets less than their fullest potential.

You are the exception. For you, there is one big difference in life; you have a dream to do something different. You want to make a difference or do something better than anyone else does. How are you going to accomplish your dreams and live to your fullest potential with all the obstacles knocking at your door? The secret is to evolve your consciousness.

Consciousness by definition means to be aware or have self-awareness. To evolve your consciousness is to follow a process that leads to an unfolding of your self-awareness — that is, the awareness of how you live and behave according to your thoughts and belief systems. And, the evolved consciousness of an entrepreneur is a mindset that allows you to transform yourself continuously into the most successful you. You can then live your life purpose, be in a state of well being and accomplish your heart's desire.

Imagine what it will be like when you are acting and living in your highest potential. Your business, branding, marketing, the operations of your company and your relationships —with yourself, your partners and employees, your audience and clients — will all flow in an effortless way. Imagine your life flowing in abundance, with the ability to see your visions clearly and to manifest your dreams into reality. That is what the evolution of your consciousness will do for you. That is why your Evolution of Consciousness is the most important piece of the puzzle, your greatest tool for success.

THE PROCESS OF AN EVOLVED CONSCIOUSNESS

So how do you become this evolved conscious mastermind of business and personal success? How do you evolve into your fullest potential? There is a guided process to give you the tools you need to clear out the old patterning and create an awakening. The steps are:

1. Acquiring the knowledge or belief that everything is energy.

The first step involves understanding and adopting the belief that you are made up of energy. Actually, everything is energy — a vibrational frequency of wave-like patterns that make up our universe. Energy is an electromagnetic charge that is within and surrounds your body Material objects are slow moving vibrational frequencies (energy) that make up matter. Thoughts are fast moving vibrational frequencies that are invisible to the naked eye, but still move and create our reality. This concept is sometimes abstract, but there is a lot of information to research at your leisure. You may want to read about The Law of Attraction or about manifesting your visions into reality. You might also watch the movie "The Secret".

As an entrepreneur, your greatest tool will be your knowledge of energy and how to manage it to master your life, your relationships and your business. Energy affects how we are in relationship to ourselves and others. It impacts how we feel on a daily basis and how our vision of life's purpose or our business is projected and manifested into the world.

For example, there are some people who, for no reason, you just cannot seem to like. They are very negative, and you feel drained when you see them. Then, there are other people who you love to be around because they are happy, have a glow about them and are especially positive. You might say it's about how they act or behave, but it is really about the energy that they put out into the world. The same goes for your business. If you know about energy you can shift the energies in your life to attract the clients you want.

Importantly, your energy moves based on your thought process. That is why they say if you have negative thoughts you will get sick. This is true. Your thoughts create energy. In an instant, you can shift your negative thoughts to positive ones. And in turn you can change your negative energy into positive energy. In sum, *"Energy goes where consciousness flows"*.

Energy is an inherent tool at your disposal; a tool that, if you choose not to use, will be there anyway, reacting to your subconscious mind, an event, which you do not want to happen in your life.

2. Grounding your energy so that you become a stable force of energy.

Life is chaos. Constantly shifting, moving and changing. There is no way to predict or control what happens in your life. This is the cause of all stress, anxiety and grief. I see life, especially during times of transformation, as a tornado swirling around you. It becomes very difficult to deal with things or to make the proper decisions (or even function, for that matter) when life is coming at you like a storm. The drama of life picks you up and lands you in any place, usually on the top of your head. And, for an entrepreneur, this tornado takes on speed and velocity, tenfold. Flying by the seat of your pants is an understatement.

If you are not careful, the decision-making process can mean life or death for your business, your dreams, your life purpose and your financial stability. Grounding your energy will allow you to be calm and stable while the chaos of life is swirling about you. You can become the calm in the center of the storm. In this calm place, you are able to see the whole picture of what is in front of you, and you will no longer be held hostage by emotional reactions to any drama. There is a centered feeling within you, and that is when you will be most effective.

In my training as a healer, I have found that grounding meditation is the foundation for any energy/healing work. You cannot be effective at moving energy if you are not grounded. You cannot make important life altering or business altering decisions if you are not grounded.

To make stable calm decisions, your energy needs to be in your body. I know that sounds a bit strange but, as humans, we have the habit of moving our energies up and outside of our physical bodies. We are not even aware of what we are doing. The energy leaves the physical body because of the emotional pain and suffering that we experience from life; it is easier to cope when we do not feel the pain.

When the energetic body is not connected to the physical form, it causes the body to feel anxious. It can cause a sense of being out of control, unsafe. This experience may cause physical symptoms like heart palpitations and other unproductive side effects. Think about a balloon on a string that is not connected to anything else. The balloon floats away. That is your energy and your consciousness floating away and, with it, the ability to function effectively.

Actually, it is extremely important to ground your energy into the earth itself. Some people have done yoga or used other techniques, such as guided meditation, and imagined roots growing from their feet into the ground. These techniques are based on centuries old teachings that say to anchor your body energy into the earth about three to four feet. There is real science behind these practices. There are electromagnetic grids in the earth's surface, and we connect the energy body into the earth's electromagnetic grids. This gives us a sense of security, belonging and calm.

In 2004, while doing my grounding techniques for meditation and healing work, I discovered a relatively new technique. I was forced to go deeper into the earth to ground my energy. I felt the connection of my energy field anchoring into something very powerful. What I have since learned is that I was anchoring into a permanent electromagnetic field of the earth. Although there is no science as of yet to validate what I was doing, through time and experience I have found this to be a very powerful grounding technique. I have taught it to many of my clients, some with stage four cancers, some facing terminal illnesses (they are in various places of instability).

I also have used this technique with my clients going through life transitions and major upheavals, as well as with those needing to feel safe and calm before making important life decisions. My clients who have used this grounding technique instantaneously felt an improved state of being. There is no waiting; the improved state of being happens as soon as you do the technique.

And, with practice, this technique becomes so easy that it is requires just a quick thought to become grounded; your consciousness and your physical body are calm, centered and balanced in a way that makes you feel safe and unaffected by what is happening around you. You will then begin to live and function through non-emotional reactions to the chaos and drama of life. This will be a great tool in your daily functioning. And, it can determine your success rate in making important business and life decisions.

To learn about this technique and how to use it on your own, please visit **(evolve2b.com…password: onlyone).**

3. Using energy to clear your negative thoughts and belief systems.

The entrepreneur is a master visionary. The spark of his or her thoughts and the dreams that they build, lead to the creation of a product or business, to fill the needs of the many. Entrepreneurs go against society's grain and the protests of the subconscious mind. Then there is the ego; everyone is watching you, secretly wanting you to fail. Or your own self-sabotage tries to take you down — not to mention how nerve-wracking it can be to make all the correct decisions about branding and marketing yourself and your business.

As an entrepreneur, your mindset must be clear and clean of any negative thoughts. Since thoughts are energy, they can literally reach out and affect your relationship with the outside world. It is, therefore, imperative that you erase any negative thoughts from your mind. Being successful is based on how well you manage and clear your thoughts, your consciousness and your energy.

So, what are negative thoughts? They are the ones that speak to you in your mind and judge everything that you do. Sometimes they are things your parents have told you, or they are based on experiences you had in the past. Some thoughts are from you, telling yourself you are not worthy, good enough, smart enough, do not have any money; the list goes on.

Then there are thoughts of your own greatness, how amazing you are and how no one can beat you or your product. Those thoughts will get you in trouble too; in business a thought can keep you from paying attention to improving your products or services.

In sum, thoughts are your ego, and your ego is a manifestation of an untruth. It is how you perceive yourself and the world based on past experiences. The ego makes up stories for us to believe and cuts us off from having an experience based in the present moment. It is the ego that will destroy your hopes and dreams. This is not ego bashing; the ego has long served you and has been a great asset in so many ways. But it has been running the "show" for your whole life. Now, to reach your fullest potential and the best life or business you can create, your ego needs to take a step back. At **evolve2b.com,** I give you a tool to clear your negative mind set gracefully, quickly and easily.

The process of the Evolution of Consciousness is the empowerment of you taking responsibility for your life. You become the master of your reality and create the life or business that you desire. When you are aware of your negative thoughts and behavior patterns, and you make the decision to let them go, you move into a place of positive thoughts, and begin to manifest a very powerful reality for yourself. This reality is filled with a presence of your own truth, living in the moment and knowing that you have the ability and tools to have what you desire.

4. Manifesting your desires from the heart.

The concept of manifesting your desires (or creating your reality) is something that has been much talked about in the past few years. When the movie, "The Secret," came out, it introduced the idea that it is possible to have the life you desire by asking for it. In fact, "The Secret" became the most popular source of information on manifesting and The Law of Attraction. What the movie doesn't mention is that this information about manifesting your desire, is based in an old paradigm (knowledge) used in a time when the earth vibrated at a different energetic frequency. There is a science to it, which you can read about in detail in my book, *Body Of Light, the Evolution of Consciousness Through the New Chakra System*.

The crucial point coming out of that science is that something about The Law of Attraction has changed and, so, the technique for manifesting has changed. Now, energy is very fast moving, and that changes the way we relate to ourselves and each other. We are coming into the world of peace; we are shifting into an era of living in our hearts. Why is that important for manifestation?

The old way to manifest was to have a vision which would shift your thoughts and move the energy to create your desires. Easy, right? It works, but is problematic in that, often, along with the thought of what you wanted, came a thought of how it might be impossible or that you are unworthy, In that case, the negative thought canceled out the vision.

The solution in this new energy is not to have a vision. Instead, go deeper, out of your mind (where the vision is) and into your heart, where your desire is. Yes, the heart is where manifestation takes place in this new era! For a great tool to teach you how to manifest from the heart and experience manifestation in this higher vibrational energy, please go to **(evolve2b.com)**.

To create and manifest what you desire into reality, it must be done from the heart. There can be no attachment to how it manifests. There is no business plan for manifestation. That is not The Law of Attraction. The Law of Attraction says like energies (thoughts move energy) attract to each other and what you desire will manifest. The most powerful energetic wave patterns are in the heart.

... the heart is far more than a simple pump ... (it is) a highly complex, self-organized information processing center with its own functional "brain" that communicates with and influences the cranial brain... These influences profoundly affect brain function and most of the body's major organs, and ultimately determine the quality of life." — **The Institute of HeartMath**

If you are going into business to create destruction or greed, the techniques I've been talking about are not for you; it won't work. Those negative emotions are low vibrational frequencies and thought forms and will no longer be tolerated in this new paradigm. However, If you are envisioning a business product or service to help make the world a better place because you know that you can improve on a system, or want to make a difference in the world and in your life, then this knowledge will work. These tools can only be used for the highest good of man.

Remember that the mind is not a perfected state of being where there are no negative thoughts. You must drop all of your vision into your heart. Breathe in your business plan — not the step-by-step process, but the end result of your goals and vision. Feel what it is like to have your successful business, all the support that you need and beyond what you can imagine. Expect that you will have the life of your dreams, feel what it's like to live in that place of complete happiness and then let it go. When negative thoughts come into your mind, use the tools I gave you to release them.

5. Stepping into the new paradigm of business and living your highest potential.

Once you have learned this process of understanding and harnessing your body energies for good, you will be able to create and manifest the business of your dreams — no, more than that — a business beyond your wildest dreams. This is especially true for entrepreneurs because coming from an evolved consciousness means that you will:

- Maintain calm and balance to make important decisions
- Clear your limiting negative thoughts and belief systems
- Living your fullest potential, vibrant and healthy — physically mentally emotional and spiritually
- Be able to manifest your desires quickly and easily

Nothing in your business, or your life, will ever be the same.

Audree Weitzman uses her knowledge and skill as a healer, reads the Akashic Records and incorporates her training in energy based life coaching into a formula she developed called Intuitive Strategies Coaching, please go to evolve2b.com for more information

Declutter Your Mind for Success

Erin Muldoon Stetson

"My baggage", "your baggage", "his baggage" —phrases thrown around in casual conversation as much as an actual suitcase is thrown around by handlers at an airport. What does it mean when we talk about our "baggage?" After all, we're not actually referring to that matching set of luggage your mother bought you after college, are we? No, we are talking about the emotional and life experience "stuff" you pick up along the way; the stuff that weighs you down and makes the inside of your head hurt.

When we take a trip, our baggage literally gets heavier and messier with each souvenir we add. And, if you're like me, you can't wait to unpack and put the dirty laundry in the wash where it belongs. Similarly, in life every experience comes with emotional as well as physical stuff. Unfortunately, not all of it is as pleasurable as the mementos from vacation. Plus, when unpacking, most of us take a look at what comes out of the suitcase so we can put it where it belongs.

But, when it comes to emotional baggage, people tend to stuff it away without really looking at it. What they are doing is filling up the emotional equivalent of a classic, overstuffed closet; the one where, when you open the door, a thousand things come crashing down on your head. The one where you don't open the door except maybe a couple inches now and then to stuff more things into the dark, scary closet.

On an emotional level, that stuffing is doing you no good at all. In fact, all that clutter is not relegated to your subconscious mind. It affects all parts of your mind, as well as your body and spirit. It causes pain, disease and emotional issues. It can block you in countless ways—from achieving your potential, living authentically and manifesting abundance in your life.

Why is your mind so cluttered in the first place? It's because you've been "collecting" experiences, memories and feelings for a lifetime. Even in the womb, there may have been alarming and confusing experiences. If you had a difficult birth, or traumatic first few moments of life, the imprint of those experiences is still with you. To add insult to injury, as a baby, you may have often struggled to be understood or to have your needs met while your bumbling care givers tried to figure out if you were hungry, sleepy or needed a diaper change. How frustrating that must have been. Those early experiences went into your collection.

Think about the clutter you have collected. I suggest that, as you read this, you jot down the thoughts that pop into your head. No doubt you will start to think of your own personal clutter that is stuffed inside you somewhere. Your notes will help you when you decide to clear that clutter out. Remember, you need to look at all of it squarely before you can put it away for good.

The collection of emotional clutter goes on throughout your life. In the toddler years, you stumble and fall (literally), and struggle to communicate only to be utterly misunderstood. Then, as a teen, you stumble figuratively as you try to find your way, and still find communication difficult as your values change in relation to those of parents, teachers or even your peers.

Think about it:

- A humiliating experience in class when a teacher scolded you in front of everyone.
- Someone you had a crush on treated you with contempt.
- A vicious, behind-the-back bullying campaign waged by an alleged "friend."
- A time when you were unkind or ungrateful to someone who didn't deserve it.
- The day you walked out of a store with a pack of gum you didn't pay for.

Each of these experiences is jarring. Every single one of them can disrupt the energy system in your body and mind. It's no wonder you feel so overwhelmed with the clutter.

I vividly remember something that happened when I was 12 years old. I received a scathing note from one of my "best friends" who happened to live across the street. It was poetic in its poignancy. "Erin, you think you're hot shit on a silver platter, but really you're just cold diarrhea on a paper plate!" Wow. That hurt. It's funny now —I mean really funny — and I'm so impressed with the verbiage. But at the time, I cried big tears —the kind of tears that I thought might never stop gushing. I had to re-think my whole persona. Did I really think that I was "hot shit?" And was I actually "just cold diarrhea?" I collected the anger, the sadness and the insecurity of that moment and buried it all in my mind, heart and body.

For the record, I'm not saying that any of the experiences I'm mentioning were bad, or good, for that matter. Nor am I saying that my friend in the "hot shit" story was wrong for writing that note. What I am saying is that our experiences stay with us, in one form or another, and often create disruptions in our energy systems.

Have you been able to jot down a few notes about memories of your own that may have stayed with you and created disruptions in your own life? Job struggles, relationship or parenting challenges, heartache, loss, trauma—the little things and the big things that may be stuffed away, buried, doing some damage unbeknownst to you.

All of these things go into your collection. Don't judge them. Don't judge yourself. Simply write down a "title" for the memory. We'll address it later and possibly let go of it with ease. You won't lose the memory, but merely the negative charge that is connected to it.

Now that you have started to examine your impressive collection, you can understand how it has grown exponentially over your lifetime. You can imagine how your mind has gotten cluttered. It's no wonder so many people feel weighed down, bottled up, distracted and even confused at times.

It is possible to declutter your mind if you have the proper tools. There is a process you can use to fix the effects of that build-up.

Pat yourself on the back for beginning this journey. It's going to be fun!

TAPPING

Tapping is based on Emotional Freedom Techniques (EFT). It is a relatively new discovery that has provided thousands with relief from pain, disease and emotional issues. It can alleviate the most common matters (fear of public speaking) to the most extreme (chronic debilitating back pain), and a wide array of "stuff" in between. Basically, tapping is mind/body healing. It is a combination of ancient Chinese knowledge and modern psychology.

Tapping produces a relaxation response in your body and mind and creates an emotional contentment in the present moment. It is wonderfully simple and effective, and it is accomplished by stimulating well established energy meridian points on your body.

"How do you do that?"

You do that by tapping on particular points with your fingertips while focusing on the issue at hand. "

Really?" "It's not more complicated than that?"

Yes, really. And no, it's not more complicated than that. Plus, the process is easy to memorize, and portable—you can do it anywhere. You only need your hands and your mind.

It is my goal to make this real healing easy and accessible to you. For the entrepreneur feeling overwhelmed, or the person who has dreams of starting a business but is blocked by fear, these techniques can help create such fundamental shifts that walls tumble and doors open. The healing path of body, mind and spirit lies ahead.

So how does tapping differ, say, from other energy healing modalities such as acupuncture? By focusing on the mind-body connection, EFT tapping harnesses the power of the mind and combines it with the body's energy to propel healing to a level that could not otherwise be achieved. The techniques essentially bring a psychotherapeutic element to the energy meridians long familiar to alternative healers.

The power of thought and its effects on our well-being are no longer considered theoretical. The evidence is piling up. So let's declutter your mind so that your thoughts no longer sabotage you but can have the impact you want them to!

EFT TAPPING IN ACTION

Let's look at a particular, very real scenario that will be familiar to many. I like to call it the fear of public writing. Now, we could also address the fear of public speaking or something else but, given the fact that I overcame my fear of public writing to write this chapter, it seems an apropos example. Additionally, the fear of public writing can be a huge deal for an entrepreneur, especially when you are expected to publish a blog, post on Facebook and update your website on a regular basis.

EFT tapping has the unique ability to handle your fears and turn them into calm cool action. Whether you feel paralyzed at the thought of doing an activity like writing, or are shy about sharing what you've already written, EFT tapping can help put those fears in check.

For example, have you hesitated to write a book because of your anxiety about the fact that the dreaded written word can never be erased? It will be "out there" speaking for you, for all time. If you are like I was, that thought paralyzes you. But here I am, writing this. And enjoying it, I might add. How am I able to face my fears so courageously?

As I mentioned above, the answer is quite simple and incredibly revolutionary. I can't wait to share this fabulous secret with you. Tap along with me. You won't be sorry. Then we can high five on the other side of this silly fear that's holding you back from your greatness.

EFT IN A NUTSHELL

The body contains a network of energy points and energy channels — actual locations that can be accessed through tapping. In addition to the physical act of tapping on these specific points, EFT involves the use of words. The power of words, of language, to channel and manifest intention is hardly in question any more. So with EFT, you will use words first to acknowledge the details of the negative — the big pieces of junk cluttering your mind.

Looking at them and facing them is the first step to releasing the junk you've been shoving into your suitcase for so long. Finally, positive language is used to manifest what you want to bring into your life after you've "put away" the clutter where it belongs. Where is that? It's where your clutter can no longer hurt you.

So, let's return to our hypothetical case of a person (maybe you) who is afraid to write. This fear is getting in the way of your business, your success and your ability to create abundance in your life. Below are the simple steps that I would walk you through if you were this hypothetical person. In no time, you would be writing and publishing.

STEP 1

Close your eyes and think about what is holding you back from writing and publishing that book or updating your blog. Once you have something specific in mind, give it a number on a scale of 0-10, ten being the most intense. If you have many things running through your mind, write them down and start with the one specific issue that has the highest intensity. Think of it as the biggest piece of junk in that closet—the one that might actually knock you out if it fell on your head. Give that piece of junk a "title"—you don't need to write down the whole sordid history or explanation of the issue, just its title. The number you assign to that issue is extremely important. It allows you to compare how you feel before and after tapping.

For example, you may be thinking: "What if my ex reads this and thinks, 'what the %&*# is she writing about? Why was I ever with that chick? What a weirdo!'" Or perhaps you are thinking, "No one who reads this will ever want to talk to me, meet me or hire me. I'll be ruined."

Your title for this piece of mental debris might be: Fear of Rejection. Maybe it earns a level of 8, 9 or even 10, depending on how paralyzing it is. (You insert whichever number makes sense for how you feel in the present moment.)

STEP 2

Tap continuously with your fingers on each of the following spots while repeating the corresponding phrases out loud. (If you think a diagram might be helpful, please visit http://taponit.com.)

Karate Chop Spot (this is the place on the side of your hand you would use if you were to use a karate chop to break a piece of wood): Tap continuously with four fingers on that spot while saying the following phrase three times aloud: "Even though I am afraid of being judged and rejected [insert here: by my ex or by future clients] for what I write, I'm still a really good person."

- **Eyebrow point** (this is the beginning of your eyebrow closest to your nose): Tap continuously with two fingers at that spot and repeat the following phrase: "I'm afraid that my [ex or future client] is going to judge me and my writing in a negative way." Repeat Once.

- **Side of eye** (this is the bone bordering the outside corner of your eye): Tap continuously with two fingers on that spot and repeat the following phrase: "What if my [ex or future client] reads what I wrote and thinks I'm a terrible writer?" Repeat Once.

- **Under the eye** (about ½ inch below): Tap continuously with two fingers, saying: "I'm nervous to put myself out there. I will be laughed at." Repeat once.

- **Under the nose** (this is the philtrum: the small indentation between the bottom of your nose and the top of your upper lip): Tap continuously with two fingers on that spot while you say: "I'm afraid that someone [my ex or a judgmental future client] is going to read my writing if I put it out there." Repeat once.

- **Chin** (the spot midway between the bottom of your chin and your lower lip): Tap continuously with two fingers on that spot and say: "I'm not sure if I can handle the embarrassment of having my writing judged by [my ex, a future client] or anyone else for that matter." Repeat once.

- **Collarbone**: Tap continuously with four fingers along your collarbone towards your breast bone. Say these words: "I'm not ready to have my thoughts and ideas critiqued and ridiculed." Repeat once.

- **Under arm** (four inches below your armpit, on the side of your body): Tap continuously with four fingers: "I'm nervous that [my ex or a future client] will read what I'm writing and make fun of me." Repeat once.

- **Crown of head**: Tap continuously with all five fingers in a circular motion on the top of your head: "I'm afraid that [my ex or anyone] is going to read my writing and laugh at me." Repeat once.

- **Eyebrow point**: "I'm okay now." Repeat once.

- **Side of eye**: "I can relax now." Repeat once.

- **Under the eye**: "I am calm and relaxed." Repeat once.

- **Under the nose**: "My confidence is growing." Repeat once.

- **Chin**: "I am feeling more and more confident about my writing." Repeat once.

- **Collarbone**: "I am excited to write an awesome [book, article, blog]." Repeat once.

- **Under arm**: "I can't wait to write my [book, article, blog]." Repeat once.

- **Top of head**: "I'm ready to write and publish an amazing [book, article, blog]." Repeat once.

When you are done, take a deep breath and hold it. Then let it out in a slow, smooth exhalation.

STEP 3

After completing the tapping and repetitions, reassess the intensity of your feelings about the topic (in this case, public writing), using the scale you used originally, from 0 to 10, with ten being the strongest. Write down your response, the number and something about how you feel. Comment about whether there were any qualitative changes to the way you view or feel about the topic. If your number is still high, then repeat the process.

Be clear in acknowledging any change. For example, "After tapping, my fear of rejection and judgment regarding my writing from [my ex or future clients] is at about a level two, down significantly from my previous level of eight."

The three steps outlined above are how you use EFT to overcome your fear of public writing. You can use the same format to cope with other issues that are holding you back. The phrases that you use in your repetitions during tapping will vary according to what you are trying to release. Here are some examples:

- **Karate Chop Spot**: "Even though I'm afraid that my family will disown me because what I want to write about is too off the grid for them, I have confidence and love. I forgive them for their potential judgments." Repeat three times.

- **Karate Chop Spot**: "Even though I fear that my ideas will change one day, and what I write will be 'out there' forever, reminding me of how foolish I was, I deeply and completely love and accept myself."

- **Karate Chop Spot**: "Even though my writing isn't perfect, it's a work in progress that never seems to end. I am whole, and complete, and fabulous just as I am right now, and so is my writing."

- **Karate Chop Spot**: "Even though I feel as if I don't have time to write, I am willing to make changes in my life because I deeply and completely love and accept myself."

The intended and very real outcome of EFT tapping in this circumstance is increased self-confidence. Whether it is your writing or something else that is standing in your way, your confidence will grow exponentially the more you tap. You will laugh at your previous fears. To use our example of fearing the reaction of your ex, once you have utilized EFT tapping, you might assume that, should he read your writing, he'll wonder how he ever let someone like you get away!

Our fears about what might happen are often times more intense than any actual, potential outcome. Tapping creates equilibrium between that fear and what is real. It will allow you to gain a calm, cool perspective regarding the debris that was weighing you down by cluttering up your suitcase or your closet –in other words, your mind!

Decluttering your mind through EFT tapping applies to literally any aspect of your life. It can help you find fulfillment, success, and enjoyment in any arena: relationships, money, body image, health etc. Starting with identifying what is holding you back, seeing it for what it is and then releasing it, you ultimately replace it with something wholesome that will help you move forward.

The things that are holding you back are all that junk we talked about earlier: Fears or objections (the "I can't" mentality), obstacles — perceived or real (time, logistics) — and ultimately your "story" – the belief system that holds you where you are instead of helping you get to where you want to be.

The process that works for your mind can also be used to declutter your body. There is a holistic connection between and among mind, body and spirit, which means that detoxing one will help you declutter the others.

Your spirit can be decluttered and detoxified too. In using EFT techniques for the spirit, you will address matters of perspective, outlook and attitude.

The law of attraction is essentially at work every time you succumb to fear or, conversely, feel optimistic. When you fear an outcome and fixate on that fear, you are focusing on what is essentially a belief system based on fear. Your mind, as well as your actions, reflects that belief system and you will manifest the very things you are afraid of.

When you can tap on and release the fear, you can recreate a belief system based on positive emotions, optimism and confidence. You become that person and your every action reflects those new beliefs.

So what does this mean for you? It means that EFT tapping can bring you more comfort, love and enjoyment in life. It can help you rid yourself of the heavy baggage and clutter that get in the way of being your most successful self.

To learn more about the benefits of tapping, please visit http://taponit.com.

Control Money Before Money Controls You

K. RAJ SINGH

My aim in contributing to this book is to inspire and motivate others through sharing my experiences – both successes and failures. My hope for you is that after reading, you realize you are just as, or even more, capable of becoming successful and having financial freedom as I have had the fortune to be. Don't get me wrong; I have had to overcome multiple obstacles in order to end up where I am in life. I believe that we don't go through mishaps and failures solely to benefit ourselves, but also so that we can impart our wisdom upon the general public and benefit humanity's quality of life as a whole.

My drive and ambition stems from growing up in a single parent household with my mother and sister. Early on in life, my parents divorced and I was given the role of man of the house. I soon found that with that title came responsibility – responsibility to provide for my family, support my family, and secure a stable financial future. Throughout this time, my ambition was in the background, ever-fueling and driving my desire for more. I wanted more for my future, more for my family, but not just in a financial sense. I've heard of so many families that struggle not financially, but emotionally, because the provider was continuously absent due to their efforts to secure a stable lifestyle for their family. I didn't want to impart that emotional burden on my family. I wanted to be there for them and not just function as their savings account or an invisible man who allows them to live a comfortable life. I wanted to be there for my sister's graduation, or my child's first steps and first words. I wanted to be present.

Being a good person and being successful are not mutually exclusive characteristics, but neither do they come hand in hand. You can be a genuinely good human being in terms of honesty and generosity, but not accomplished in terms of achieving your career goals. In order to become who I wanted to be for my family, I had to learn how to be both the best and most successful person I had the potential to be. To do this, I attended multiple seminars and workshops on personal development, investing, and financial success. To this day, I still continue to learn and grow as a person with every day I live, but one seminar has had a significant impact on my financial life, specifically. This was Peak Potentials' Millionaire Mind Intensive by T. Harv Eker (now called New Peaks' Millionaire Mind Experience*). The Millionaire Mind Intensive seminar taught me not to just wonder why life is the way it is and imagine my position in life as static, but to start asking myself how I could change my financial blueprint and future. And that's exactly what I did.

I am now in a global mastermind group with New Peaks and feel blessed to have been able to spend time with the CEO, Adam Markel, who is also author of the book Pivot. I've visited him in his home in California, where we spent hours brainstorming ideas and solutions for our businesses, while also making time for fun and giving back to a worthy cause with our time and physical labor. The dedication that Mr. Markel and the rest of his team put into their company is wondrous and admirable. I, along with countless other people, have taken many of the courses and retreats they offer – my favorite being the Enlightened Warrior Training Camp. The name alone says a lot about the focus of the retreat as becoming an enlightened warrior means to conquer oneself.

As I mentioned before, I wanted to figure out a way to be financially successful but also be present for my family. The best way I have found to do this was to delegate and relinquish some control. For some people this may be hard, especially the types that are perfectionists and relish the ability to oversee every detail of any operation. But in order for me to have enough free time to spend with my family and loved ones, I had to realize that a significant amount of the work I did myself could be distributed and done by other people. I began to hire others to do the more routine work I had grown accustomed to doing myself and although at first glance this seemed like a big initial investment, I soon reaped its benefits. Not having to do the work of multiple people allowed me to focus on the more complex aspects of the projects I was working on and with greater focus came increased levels of productivity. That's when the successes started rolling in.

None of the headway I made after bringing in others to help would have been possible if I hadn't realized the importance of continued education, even after obtaining my Bachelor's Degree. This doesn't necessarily have to mean taking online classes or auditing courses at your local college – it can be as simple as reading an article on a topic you don't know much about or taking a weekend and attending a seminar on smart investing. Having a vast store of a variety of information allows you to be creative in your problem solving and future planning, as you can take multiple viewpoints when looking at the situations you find yourself in. "Knowledge is power" isn't a famous quote just because the sound of the words is aurally appealing; there is innate truth in those three words, dating back to 1597 in Sir Francis Bacon's Meditationes Sacrae. As you can see, this book isn't just about investing in stocks or bonds; rather it's about investing in yourself – your education, your future, and your success. To take it a step further, I believe knowledge, when applied, is power. Warren Buffet, the biggest investor of our time, says: "The best investment you can make is an investment in yourself… The more you learn, the more you'll earn." I've noticed throughout my life that wealthy people tend to always have extensive libraries in their homes and I firmly believe there is a correlation between their success and the importance they put on accumulating knowledge. Knowledge, and the ability of correctly applying it, are the greatest assets in the world because the dividends are infinite.

*As a thank you for purchasing this book, I am offering a scholarship certificate for you and a family member to attend the 3-day Millionaire Mind Experience Seminar as my complimentary guests. Valued at $2,590 – free for a limited time! Go to www.thepassiveincomebook.com

THE LAW OF ATTRACTION

The law of attraction ultimately boils down to the idea that "like attracts like." In a way, our thoughts are made up of energy, just as we are, and whether our thoughts are positive or negative can determine whether we encounter positive or negative experiences. The idea of similar energy types attracting each other, also known as the law of attraction, was brought to fame and popularity through Rhonda Byrne's book-turned-movie, The Secret. I was blessed to come across this book at a pivotal point in my life and owe most of my beliefs to the lessons I took from reading it. I truly believe it to be the single most powerful and impactful piece of literature I have studied. When I met the greatest motivational speaker, Anthony Robbins*, I learned that all of us have a vibrational energy, and in order to succeed, we need to increase our energy levels to the maximum we can obtain. The more energy we have, the more of what we want from the universe we can attract. You can think of it in terms of gravity – bigger bodies of matter have bigger gravitational pulls, and ultimately attract larger amounts of mass. The sun is a good example of this. Surrounded by eight planets, a dwarf planet, and countless asteroids, the sun is a giant orb, pulsing of energy and attracting an incredible amount of matter towards it. We should all try to draw as much positive energy towards ourselves as possible.

An efficient way to attract favorable energy is to actively maintain a positive attitude every day. I cannot stress enough how important I have found having a positive attitude to be. Especially since we live in a world where negative happens all around us, this may initially be harder than it seems but with conscious effort, staying positive can become habit. To help you visualize this, I want you to imagine a field of dirt. Without doing anything or putting in any effort, grass and weeds will take it over and destroy its potential. However, by planting your own crops and nurturing them with fertile soil and water, you can eventually end up with a bountiful field full of fruits or vegetables. With effort, the positive has overcome the default negative. In this same way, actively trying to maintain a positive attitude can help you eliminate the negative that regrettably encompasses the world.

A more tangible way to do this in your daily life is to listen to personal development and motivational audio books in your spare time. I used to use the time I spent commuting to work to do this; I even called my car my "University on Wheels." No matter where I was going, I was always able to feel as if I'd done something productive, other than driving from point

A to point B. If audio books aren't up your alley, you could also opt for the real paper version of the books. Reading every night before bed has become a deeply embedded habit for me, and I regard it as a habit everyone should develop. Most people spend their last minutes before sleep watching the news on TV, something full to the brim with negativity. "If it bleeds, it leads" is a common phrase that comes to mind when we think about the news – is that something really the last thing we want to be exposed to before sleeping? Our mind will slowly fade away from consciousness as we fall asleep, but our subconscious is still processing all of the violence and blood we witnessed through the TV. I equate watching the news before bed with letting someone come into your home and throw garbage everywhere right before you leave the house. Don't let something as negative as a newscast filled with misfortune and violence fill your mind right before sleep. Alternatively, think about if you were to just read a few pages of a motivational book before going to bed – the last words you experience before sleep are now something positive and propelling. You wake up feeling refreshed and energized the next morning, ready to tackle whatever challenges you may face that day.

A good tactic I have found for achieving success and a positive attitude is to find a person who is successful in the way you want to be and to study them. As I mentioned before, continuing education is an important part of achieving your goals, and studying people is yet another way you can learn to improve. I've had countless mentors over the years and even a life coach to help me through the happy and more complicated times. Each of these people has impacted my life in different ways, as every one of them had different experiences and types of knowledge to offer. I consciously recognize that without these people, I would be nowhere near the place where I am today. I am also able to realize that not only have these people helped me get to where I am now, but also my past mistakes have been integral to my success.

I firmly stand by the idea that we are all in the right place at the right time. Even though things may seem difficult at that specific time, or you may fail once or twice or several times, everything that happens to you is meant to happen. No matter the situation, there is always a lesson you can learn from your experiences.

Your income will never exceed your self-image of how great you perceive yourself to be, therefore you must grow your self-image alongside self-improvement to feel truly worthy of a greater income. In order to better visualize my goals, I created a vision board. A vision board can be something as simple as a poster with pictures of things you want in your future, regardless of what facet of life they pertain to. I love staring at my vision board and feeling excited about living in that reality. I encourage everyone to ponder over their vision board every day and visualize living that life in the present so you can attract it. It's a rewarding feeling that I can't properly put into words when you're able to start watching yourself achieve those goals and subsequently replacing them with new dreams. Some of the things I've achieved from my vision board are owning a new Mercedes Benz, meeting Billionaire Sir Richard Branson* at the iconic Playboy Mansion, meeting Mogul P. Diddy*, having a library for others to learn from, invited to Tai Lopez's $16 Million Mansion in Beverly Hills*, owning different passive income businesses I'll discuss later in the chapter, and so many more.

Going along with the idea that exuding positive energy attracts more positive energy, I believe that gratitude is one of the most powerful forces of the universe. Being grateful in life attracts more things to be grateful for. I believe if the ability to feel gratitude is not learned on the way up, then it will surely be learned on the way down. To make sure I have agency in expressing and being aware of the things I'm grateful for, I often write in my Gratitude Journal before I go to sleep at night. Essentially it is a list of all the things I feel blessed to have in life overall, specifically for that day, and specifically in that moment.

Unfortunately, most people are used to thinking about all the things in life they are unhappy about. They subsequently focus on and put passion into those things to try and fix them which is a recipe for more disaster. Rather than counting their blessings, they're counting their problems. Once you find a way to deliberately focus on all of your blessings, more of them will come to you and you will ultimately be happier in life. As I like to say, "the Pessimist may be more accurate, but the Optimist lives longer and happier."

A way that I have found to remain positive and focused on my blessings is having sessions with my life coach, whom I've had for over a decade now. Our sessions have consisted of a half an hour phone call every 2 weeks for over the last 10 years. My life coach, Dr. Elena Pezzini, helps me to set realistic goals and holds me accountable to them. She also is always making sure all areas of my life are in balanced harmony with each other and steers me in the right direction if I am lacking in an area of health, wealth, family, relationships, business, sociality, or spirituality. She always reminds me how important it is to celebrate my successes.

Alongside Dr. Pezzini, I have a sort of personal advisory board I go to on different subjects. In addition to paying for my professional life coach, I have a vocal coach for singing, spiritual advisors, specialty business mentors, and a therapist, all of whom I consult with regularly. A key point here is to pay for it – especially with life and business advisors, you get what you pay for, and when you have some skin in the game you value it more. If you are the smartest person in the room, then you're in the wrong room. You are a product of your environment and surrounding yourself with those who you perceive as more intelligent or successful will cause you to strive to be more like them. Swami Paramhansa Yogananda gave us the aphorism, "environment is stronger than will power." The Ramayan scripture states that when you are surrounded with a certain company you will then be like that company. Is your surrounding harvesting your growth?

*See my pictures with Anthony Robbins, teachers featured in The Secret, Sir Richard Branson, Tai Lopez, etc. at www.thepassiveincomebook.com

MY PAST REAL ESTATE SUCCESS STORIES

Fortunately for me, my success story featured on a National Cable & Television broadcast on the Cash Flow Generator infomercial* when I earned a six-figure profit after only my first year in real estate. This, in part, allowed me to jumpstart my success in the real estate industry and eventually at the height of my involvement in the field, I had managed hundreds of tenants across multiple buildings. In the years preceding and following this time, I learned many lessons. The most important ones I learned, though, involved how to compromise and deal with people who weren't always willing to meet in the middle. No matter what field you work in or where you live in the world, you will always come across people who truly believe that they are always right in their opinions or mindsets. Being exposed to this type of personality so early on in my professional life allowed me to use the tactics I gained throughout my property managing days to more efficiently deal with my future bosses, employees, and investors. People-managing skills are amongst the most relevant that you can gain.

Overseeing numerous buildings also meant constantly having to maintain the infrastructure and quality of dwellings. Often enough, a new problem arose – burst pipes, new carpeting needed, leaky ceilings – you name it, I probably dealt with it. These problems had me in consistent contact with contractors, plumbers, electricians, and handymen in general. A majority of the contractors I dealt with were exceedingly unreliable, and this caused me many a setback in getting my apartments move-in-ready. The more time my properties were vacant, the more money I lost. Thankfully I had some financial leeway because of the income my other properties brought in, but for someone with not as many properties, an inefficient contractor could mean the difference between a successful investment in a rental property or a failure. Take your time in choosing whom you work with in maintaining or renovating your building, and always budget for possible money lost if the project takes longer than expected (which it always does).

Unfortunately, alongside difficult tenants and fickle contractors, I also had to deal with lawsuits. Fraud, discrimination in screening applicants, and physical injury on the property are among the most common problems I had to deal with. Fortunately, I ran my properties with the utmost care and honesty, so none of the lawsuits I personally encountered ever succeeded in their intentions. Yet another lesson I can impart upon you relates to that – be honest in your dealings and avoid shortcuts. Even though these things may seem like they provide an immediate benefit, in the long run they are detrimental to your success. In the late 60s, psychologist Walter Mischel led a series of experiments on delayed gratification, which were subsequently named the Stanford Marshmallow Experiments. In these experiments, a young child was given the choice between being able to eat one marshmallow immediately or waiting 10-15 minutes and being able to eat two marshmallows. Decades later, Mischel followed up with the children from the original studies and measured multiple facets of success. Ultimately, the children who were able to delay gratification for a bigger reward down the line were more successful in multiple areas of life, including both professional success and being able to maintain a healthy lifestyle. You can see from this study that success is correlated to one's ability to see into the future and realize that maybe the quickest reward is not the best.

*See the Infomercial video clip at www.thepassiveincomebook.com

MY PAST INVESTMENT HISTORY

Although investing can have its advantages, it can also be harmful if you aren't careful or attentive with your investments. It also isn't an immediate profit that you earn if you choose to stick with it for the long run, rather than day trading or choosing more short-term investments. Look at the stock market – it varies day-to-day, month-to-month, and year-to-year. Some stocks can increase generously in the matter of weeks while others can take much longer to see the same increase in return. There is no guarantee, either, that you will make money off of your investment, regardless of how accomplished your investment manager is. Companies are unpredictable, as there are so many things that can contribute to their value, and sometimes despite your best efforts and time spent researching, an investment can go the opposite way intended.

A few companies that I invested in ultimately ended up shutting down before I could cash out my funds, and I had to quickly rebalance my finances when faced with these unexpected losses. These setbacks taught me to more carefully weigh the risks and benefits of the investment portfolios I considered, even if it took up a little more of my time than I intended. I viewed these losses as obstacles I had to overcome and didn't let them discourage me from future investments, if a seemingly profitable one came across my path.

Another business venture that aided in my financial success was my involvement in network marketing businesses, also known as multi-level marketing. You've probably heard of a few of these – Amway is one of the better-known network marketing businesses I was heavily involved in, as well as Prepaid Legal Services (now called Legal Shield), and Javita. The basic idea of these types of companies is that an individual buys in to the company and can earn commission on the products that they end up selling. This type of "employment" allows you to be flexible in your hours, work from home, and essentially be your own boss. They typically require a minimal initial investment to get a sample of the product you're selling and to gain a feel for how to market it when you start selling to other people. This type of business venture usually attracts people who are looking for flexible employment and if you can dedicate enough time and effort, it can end up being quite the lucrative option. The personal development and leadership ability gained here in their proven system are priceless.

My father would say to me that you should have 3 types of people in your life: 1) someone greater than you to learn from, 2) someone at your level to exchange ideas with, and 3) someone younger than you to teach what you've learned. Network Marketing provides an opportunity for all 3 with your up-line, down-line, and sideline people.

DISCOVER YOUR PASSION

An easy way to discover what you're truly passionate about is to take a step back and look at your hobbies. Hobbies are what you choose to do in your free time and are things you genuinely enjoy, rather than being something you feel obligated to do because it provides for your family or allows you to lead an extravagant lifestyle. You will be most successful in endeavors that you're passionate about since working towards your goals won't seem like work.

Unfortunately, sometimes your hobbies don't necessarily match up with what kind of income you need in life. That's when you try your best to find a career field that you can be successful in, while also making time to do the things you truly enjoy. Maintaining a consistent effort towards having one or two interests outside of work will help keep you feeling satisfied with where you are in life.

Another way to work towards becoming the most successful person you can be is looking at why you do the things you do. I've noticed throughout my life that as long as you're doing something for the right reasons, things will generally fall in your favor. Why you're doing something ultimately determines how you do it. If you start something with good intentions, you will put in the effort necessary for making sure your goals come to fruition. On the other hand, if you work towards something but with the wrong intentions, you may still become successful, although there is a smaller chance of that and your achievements may not feel as satisfying as if why you did that was for a purer reason. This is yet another reason why you should look at your hobbies and try your hardest to find a career that matches up with them. If what you end up doing for the rest of your life is something you're truly passionate about, then you will have become the most successful person you can be.

For me, my passions have to do mainly with the arts and performing in front of an audience of thousands of people locally and internationally. My favorite quote is from the movie Braveheart "Everyone dies, but not everyone truly lives." I feel truly alive when I sing with my band on stage, act on stage for charity, emcee events, and even do TV/Radio interviews. All of these were done alongside my investments in the stock market, FOREX market, and real estate, and they helped me maintain a feeling of being creative, something I truly cherish. Even though I didn't make a full-time career out of any of my hobbies, I was still able to pursue them because I found a way to run my business efficiently and have enough free time. Without a way to express my creative side, I most likely would have failed at most of the goals I tried to achieve career-wise as I would have felt confined in a world where I wasn't able to be completely myself.

I also derive satisfaction from contributing back to my community or the world I live in through charity work. To some people this can mean writing a check for some non-profit organization, while for others it can mean being directly involved with the charity through volunteering or being on the board. Some have the time for the latter while for most all they can contribute is a small monetary donation. I love the Sai Baba quote that says "Hands that serve mankind are holier than lips that pray". I find as long as I'm able to lend a helping hand in some way, I feel as if I've done some good with my life. However, I do advise you take caution with the charities you choose to invest in, as some don't actually give back as much as the general public thinks they do.

Luckily enough for me, even though it may have happened upon me later in life than I preferred, I found something I was genuinely passionate about that I could also make money off of. That was investing on a diverse scale. I loved the continual education that was required of investing. I always had to know what was going on in the market or in foreign economies so that I could try and predict which of my investments was going to become profitable, or which ones I should just cut my losses with. I then started hiring people smarter than me. I ended up loving it so much that I chose to start my own private investment club and became the go-to guy for people that wanted ideas about passive income investing. I have faith and hope that everyone in life will eventually be able to find an opportunity to be successful and happy like I have, even if it may cross your path when you least expect it.

PASSIVE INCOME

Passive income is part of the idea of unearned income; essentially, it is income that is received on a consistent basis with minimal effort put in to manage and maintain it. You can receive unearned or passive income from things such as pensions, inheritance, and property income, which don't require any active effort to profit from. These types of earnings are what people typically become wealthy from, rather than the salary they earn from their day jobs. Instead of living directly off of their earnings from their day jobs, many people can cut down on their daily expenses and use those savings to invest in opportunities that allow them to earn a passive income.

The most common ways to earn passive income are through rental and investment income. Rental income initially is not purely passive income, as the initial down payment and maintenance of the property can require a lot of time and effort depending on the state and quality of the building or buildings you choose to purchase. Even after this initial investment, there is still a consistent effort that needs to be put in for rental properties to maintain profitability. You have to collect checks from every tenant each month (which may not always go through) and deal with a multitude of problems that arise from difficult tenants or neighbors, or even from the infrastructure of the building itself. Rental income, however, is more a passive income than your day job, and can sometimes even be more profitable if managed in an efficient way.

In contrast, investment income is on the opposite spectrum of passive income and requires little effort after the initial investment to start earning profit. However, sometimes investing necessitates quite a large chunk of money to begin earning even a small percentage of gain. Looking at just profiting from dividends, which are payments made by a corporation to its shareholders, to make even $1,000 a year with a 4% annual dividend payout (a pretty hefty payout) you have to invest $25,000. In cases like these, it's best to do your research beforehand and find which companies are slotted to be the most profitable in the next year, as they use a fraction of their retained earnings as dividends to shareholders. The more profit a company earns, the more it can pay out to its shareholders.

There are other ways you can earn passive income through investing, too. You can trade commodities, stocks, currencies on the foreign exchange market (FOREX), securities, and even precious metals. I hire FOREX traders who I know that leverage my time so that I don't have to trade myself, or monitor the global news reports constantly. Each of these options has their advantages and drawbacks, but they are all considered a type of passive income. One of the more frequently chosen of the aforementioned options is investing in a mutual fund, which is professionally managed and pools money from multiple investors to purchase securities. This type of investment is most useful in planning for retirement, as it has a decreased amount of risk compared to investing in individual securities since a fund typically holds a diverse portfolio of securities. If one of the securities in the fund doesn't do well, chances are at least a few others did well enough to make up for the loss attributable to that one security. However, mutual funds come with fees when you buy and sell shares and are already "pre-packaged." This means you don't have as much freedom to customize your investment portfolio as you would have investing in individual securities yourself.

Another way I have found to earn passive income is through tax lien certificates. A lien is a type of security over a property to ensure that the owner pays back any debt or obligation they owe to the lien holder. A tax lien certificate, specifically, is for when a property has a lien placed upon it due to unpaid property taxes. They ultimately represent the right to foreclose on a property when there is failure of property tax payments. These certificates can be auctioned off to investors, who pay the amount of taxes owed on the property in order to then gain the right to collect the unpaid taxes from the owners plus the current rate of interest on tax lien certificates. These rates can range anywhere from 5 to 36 percent and the property owner has a period of 6 months to 3 years to pay back the taxes and interest. If the owner fails to do so by the end of the redemption period, then the lien holder is allowed to start foreclosure proceedings and take ownership of the property. Either way, with careful consideration of which tax lien certificates you choose to buy, you could earn a fair amount of passive income. However, you must figure out what your responsibilities are concerning obtaining ownership of the lien – in some states, you are required to send multiple letters at different time points notifying the owners that you now own the lien and if they fail to repay their taxes, you can foreclose on their property. Some even have expiration dates where if you don't initiate foreclosure proceedings within a certain time after the redemption period, you no longer have the right to the property. All in all, tax lien certificates have the potential to be highly profitable if you can do the research required of them.

A less well-known method of generating passive income is through owning or leasing ATM machines. The way to make a passive income through this is with the service fee that most ATMs impose upon the user. Typically, these range anywhere from $2-$5 and with each transaction on the machine, that is what you end up earning. Although it may seem like a miniscule amount at first glance, imagine if just 10 people a day used your machine. At the low end of service fees, that still equates to $600 a month with you essentially doing nothing. First off, you have to make the decision to either purchase or lease an ATM machine. Even though purchasing an ATM requires a larger initial investment, it is ultimately less expensive than leasing a machine, as you own it outright rather than having to pay a monthly fee to use and profit from it. There are some legal hoops that you may have to jump through, though, such as registering the ATM machine with your county clerk if you plan on running it under a business' name. After you ensure you have all the proper licenses, you can start placing the ATM machines in carefully picked locations, which is ultimately what matters most when trying to profit from this type of venture. You want to guarantee that your ATM is placed in an area that receives enough foot traffic and is far away enough from a bank that it is more convenient for people to withdraw money from your ATM than the bank.

Finally, the last approach I'll mention here to generating passive income that I have personally done and can suggest is through product sourcing or drop shipping. Product sourcing is a way to sell items on eBay or Amazon where the sellers never actually handle the item and instead it is sent directly from the warehouse to the buyer. The sellers of the products purchase in bulk from the warehouse, but the warehouse holds the items for the seller and then ships it out when a buyer purchases a unit. By buying in bulk, the seller is able to receive a discount on the item, which they can then choose to sell full price to the buyer. This is essentially where your profit comes from through product sourcing. There are some disadvantages to this method though – most notably is the fact that drop shippers frequently run out of stock of their more popular items, which the seller doesn't find out until after they sell the item and notify the supplier that it needs to be shipped. This results in bad feedback for your store on eBay, and can decrease the amount of traffic you end up getting. In addition, there has recently been a rise in drop shippers exporting directly from China – essentially drop shippers are now directly selling their product on eBay themselves. This is a difficult market to enter specifically on eBay, as shoppers on this website are typically looking to strike a bargain, while you're looking to make a profit. Furthermore, some suppliers don't offer the true wholesale price on their products when you're buying on the minimum side of a bulk order. However, if you're able to establish a satisfying professional relationship with your drop shipper, and ensure that you're getting a real wholesale price, then this type of venture could be profitable.

PRIVATE INVESTMENT CLUBS

In order to benefit my friends, family, and business partners as much as possible, I started a private investment club to educate them using the experience I've gained in over the past decade. The diversity of ventures I've pursued and achieved success in makes me a unique and extensive expert on passive income. Through all of my trials and errors, I've finally figured out ways to make money work for me, rather than me working for money. I want to be able to share that knowledge with as many people as possible, which is why I decided to write this book.

If you are an accredited investor or a sophisticated investor and get accepted into a private investment club, it truly can be a passive investment – you don't need to work to earn any profit. On my website, www.thepassiveincomebook.com, you can read testimonials and referrals from multiple different people who have chosen to learn smart investing ideas and strategies with me. Like me, they're able to spend less time trying to earn money and worrying about it, and more time living a passion-filled life.

Additionally, I work with a group of commercial investors that invest in multi-family apartment building units in emerging markets and help people get a higher than average rate of return secured by real estate in the USA. I've learned about this type of commercial investing directly from Real Estate Guru David Lindahl and his mentorship program. There are so many cash flow and equity position opportunities available to someone as a private lender. Private loans can be loaned to a real estate investor and secured by real estate for rehabilitation projects, flips, or rental holdings. Private loan investors are given a first, or a second mortgage, that secures their legal interest in the property and secures their investment. "Secured" means that their money is secured by an asset, which in this case is the real estate property.

Many people don't realize that they can even invest their retirement income into real estate and other investments themselves, tax-free. You can roll it over and not get charged any penalties with a self-directed IRA. This can be an incredible way to leave a legacy for generational wealth.

RISKS, CAUTION, AND SAFETY

Like with any new adventure, there is inherent risk in investing your money in the ways I've previously mentioned. With investing, there are two basic types of risk – systematic and unsystematic. Systematic is a type of risk that you are unable to avoid when investing and it can affect a broad spectrum of assets. A good example of a systematic risk would be an important political event that could possibly influence the entire market. On the other hand, unsystematic risk, or specific risk, only affects a small number of assets. For example, if union workers from the port were to strike, then only stocks for companies that dealt with that port would be affected. Thankfully though, unlike systematic risk, you can protect yourself from unsystematic risk through diversification. The more diverse an investment portfolio you have, the more you can ensure that a drop in one stock doesn't equate to a drop in your entire portfolio, since you have different kinds of stocks that can make up for that loss. However, there is a tradeoff between risk and return – higher risk stocks typically have a higher payout while lower risk stocks tend to have a lower return. This is where you have to ask yourself, how much are you willing to gamble? Do you have the freedom to take a loss or are you still too early on in your financial journey to afford that potential loss? I want you to use the lessons from this book to be able to get yourself to a point where you feel comfortable occasionally taking those risks to get a higher payout. As long as you don't continuously invest in high-risk stocks or securities and make smart investments, you could have the opportunity to receive a high return.

I do want to caution you though. No matter how much you diversify your portfolio, the risk of investing will never be zero. You can, however, reduce it as much as possible through diversification. This doesn't just mean making sure to invest in different types of companies, but also different types of investment vehicles. There are stocks, mutual funds, real estate, foreign currency, and bonds, among other things. Choosing multiple vehicles across various industries ensures that if one takes a dive, it's more than likely that your other investments are safe and sound. A not well-known way to diversity your portfolio to reduce risk is to also vary the risk of your investments. To minimize risk, you don't have to commit yourself to only choosing blue chip stocks or other types of vehicles with very low risk. If you pick investments with varying rates of return, you can help guarantee that a high return will make up for any losses in other industries or vehicles.

If you feel like you don't have enough free time to initially commit to diversifying your own portfolio, you can always trust a professional to cultivate your portfolio for you, or invest your money in an already-created and vetted portfolio. This chapter has been all about how to make money work for you so that you have financial freedom, and as I said before, a good way to start is to delegate and get educated. So why don't you take that next step? Start investing and share with me your personal success stories and breakthroughs. Contact us today to learn more about our informational products and seminars.

To read more about K. Raj Singh's experiences and wisdom, get his newest book titled "Control $, Before $ Controls You: Finding Your Passion Through Passive Income" and visit www.thepassiveincomebook.com

www.ingramcontent.com/pod-product-compliance
Lightning Source LLC
Chambersburg PA
CBHW070240190526
45169CB00001B/249